SOTHIS PRESS

Sothis Press aims to completely reimagine the public domain book with an emphasis on universal access to captivatingly designed print editions. We believe that technology will enable every single book ever published to be perpetually accessible in beautiful print form. Sothis is beauty in ubiquity.

www.sothis.press

1 Waterhouse Square, London, ECIN 2ST

Petroleum in California

A Concise and Reliable History of the Oil Industry
of the State; Containing Facts and Figures
Carefully Compiled and Information That
Can Be Obtained in No Other Form

lionel V. Redpath

SOTHIS PRESS

ISBN 978-1-0365-2445-6

This edition is published by
Sothis Press © 2023. The company
is registered in England and Wales.
The Company Number is 14900389.

PETROLEUM
IN
CALIFORNIA

A CONCISE AND RELIABLE HISTORY

OF THE

OIL INDUSTRY OF THE STATE

Contains Facts and Figures Carefully Compiled and
Information that can be obtained
in no other form

ALL PERSONS INTERESTED
IN PETROLEUM DEVELOPMENT WILL FIND THIS WORK INVALUABLE
AND INDISPENSABLE

COMPILED AND PUBLISHED BY
LIONEL V. REDPATH, 405 Blanchard Building, Tel. Black 1346, Opp. City Hall,
LOS ANGELES, CAL., U. S. A.

INTRODUCTION

Nature has been lavish with her gifts in California. The gods of fabled lore have here poured forth their riches in exhaustless profusion. From the day when the first hardy explorer set foot on the golden sands of the Pacific to this, the grandest year in the history of the commonwealth, the tale of California's greatness has been a constantly unfolding panorama of glad surprises and increased treasures.

California's gold, which poured in a steady yellow stream into the nation's coffers for more than half a score of years prior to the breaking out of the civil war, made it possible for the nation to maintain its credit and bring the war to a successful termination.

California's fruit is the wonder and delight of the civilized world, and California's wine, when shipped across the ocean, comes back to us as the choicest vintage of sunny France.

Where gold and fruit have stood in the past, in the category of the State's industries and wealth, there also will the production of oil stand in the future—a mighty triumvirate! Scientific oil men are firm in the belief that the industry is only in its infancy, and that the production will exceed in the future the production of any known oil fields on this continent. The explored oil territory is now being worked at intervals for a distance of four hundred miles, and the time will come when the State will be traversed by a line of oil derricks extending from San Diego to Siskiyou.

In order that information of this great new industry may be furnished to the people of the world in convenient form, which will be valuable for reference, and in order to send abroad, where the tale of California's wonderful riches in oil are just now beginning to attract attention, a reliable and comprehensive statement of "Petroleum in California," this volume has been issued.

CONTENTS

BEAUTIFUL SCENE IN THE KERN RIVER FIELD, A RESERVOIR OF OIL. SHOWING WELLS OF THE AZTEC OIL COMPANY.

Views in
Sunset
McKittrick
and
Kern River
Oil Fields

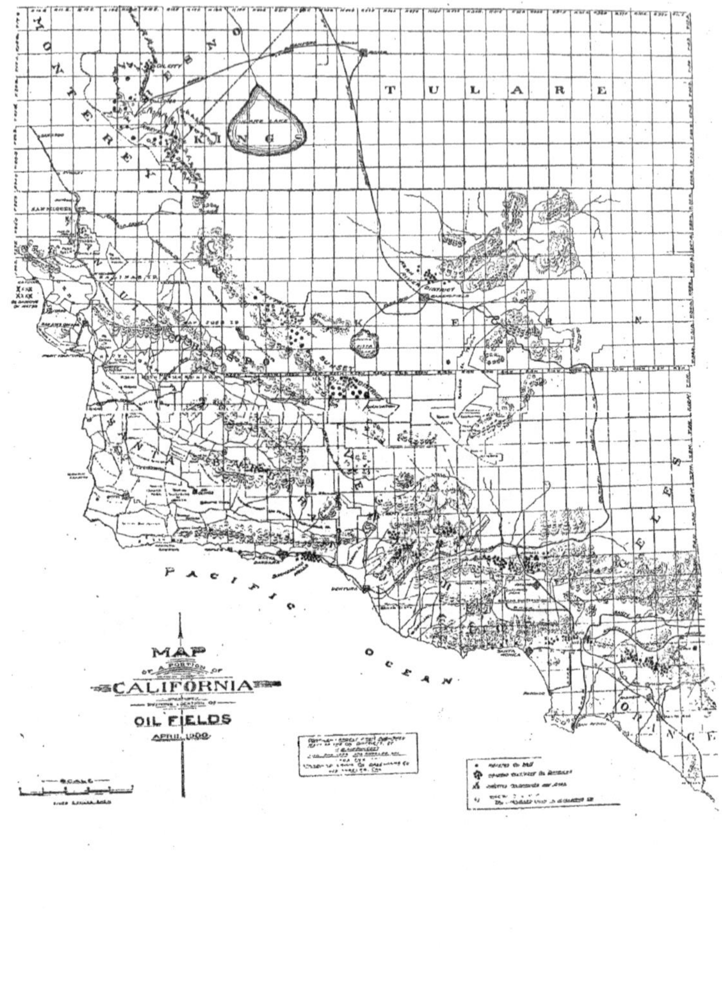

MAP
OF A PORTION OF
CALIFORNIA
OIL FIELDS
APRIL
TULARE
KINGS
MONTEREY
KERN
PACIFIC
OCEAN
ORANGE
SCALE

HISTORICAL

WHILE the production of crude petroleum is referred to as California's "new" industry, the fact that it is not classed among the old industries of the state is not the fault of the hardy sons of the state, through whose efforts the structure of the commonwealth was builded. Almost from the first settlement of the state, the existence of oil springs has been known. Deposits of asphaltum have been worked and brea beds have been utilized both for fuel and for paving purposes. The following historical sketch will give some idea of the earlier attempts to utilize petroleum in California. It is taken from a paper read by Prof. W. L. Watts of the State Mining Bureau before the American Institute of Mining Engineers, visiting Los Angeles last year.

"The existence of petroleum in California has been known for many years. From time immemorial the California Indians used this mineral, in the form of asphaltum, for various purposes. In the early history of the state the Catholic fathers utilized it for roofing their missions and other buildings.

"It is said that in 1855 or '56, Andreas Pico distilled petroleum on a small scale for the San Fernando Mission. He obtained his crude oil from Pico canyon, near Newhall in Los Angeles county; and he was probably the first refiner of petroleum in the state. In 1856 a company commenced work at La Brea ranch in Los Angeles county, and tried to refine the crude oil. In 1857 an attempt was made to produce illuminating oil from crude petroleum at Carpinteria in Santa Barbara county; and there are records of similar attempts having been made in other localities previous to 1860, but none of them were successful.

"The first scientific report of petroleum in California was made by Prof. B. Silliman who published his researches in 1865. He spoke favorably of obtaining petroleum in remunerative quantities in this state, and gave the results of his experiments on the fractional distillation of California petroleum.

"The next decade was marked by a considerable oil excitement in California, and a great many companies were formed for the purpose of petroleum mining, and for distilling crude oil.

"In most instances these companies did not meet with success, but it must be remembered that the pioneer oil miners did not have the drilling machinery of the present day, and that they only possessed limited knowledge concerning the geological conditions pertaining to the occurrence of petroleum deposits.

"The pioneer distillers appear to have expected that by the fractional distillation of California petroleum, they would obtain similar products to those resulting from the fractional distillation of the petroleum found in the Eastern States; but they were disappointed. It is not surprising that in the course of years the smaller operators became merged in larger concerns.

In 1887 when the State Mining Bureau made a reconnaissance of the petroleum industry of California, the only companies actually engaged in petroleum mining were: The Pacific Coast Oil Company in Pico canyon, and the Puente Oil Company, in the Puente hills, Los Angeles county; the Hardison & Stewart Oil Company subsequently incorporated as the Union Oil Company of Ventura county, and McPherson & Co. who were operating on Moody Gulch in Santa Clara county.

"The first refinery that can be considered a commercial success, was that of the California Star Oil Company, which was situated near Newhall, in Los Angeles county, and managed by T. H. Scott. Subsequently, refineries were erected at Alameda by the Pacific Coast Oil Company, and at Santa Paula by the Union Oil Company. At the present day there are refineries at Los Angeles, Chino, Ventura, and Alameda, also at Oleum in Contra Costa county, to which place the refinery of the Union Oil Company was removed."

EARLY OIL EXCITEMENT IN CALIFORNIA

In order to give some idea of the extent of the excitement which the early explorations assumed and the large amount of territory prospected at that time, the following article from the Pacific Oil Reporter is presented. The article has evidently been compiled with great trouble and pains. The Reporter says:

"If oil men want to talk of wild-catting, excitements, rushes, fake companies, etc., in the California oil field they ought to go back to the state's first oil excitement in 1864 or thereabouts. Everything in these lines in these later days pales to stupidity in the lurid light of the oil craze that attended the birth of the petroleum industry. There is much highly interesting reading in the files of the California papers in the early sixties. Few remember much about those oil times, and to most oil men of this generation the oil items of those days are just like news.

"The great oil excitement that followed the discovery at Oil City, Pa., and the ones that followed in that Eastern region naturally soon drew attention to the many oil indications in California, and as naturally set fire to every seepage from Santa Barbara to Humboldt. The crazy exploitation of oil companies in the East was quickly attended by similar operations here. Little was known about petroleum then, and the speculations of intelligent people, and even the theories of scientists, sound strangely absurd now. The most extravagant ideas attended the most extravagant financial operations at a time when fortunes were being made and lost by "Coal Oil Johnnies" on a remarkable scale. So the furor over the oil indications of California early followed and amalgamated with the Eastern craze, and in some ways was even more extravagant. It was red hot in 1864, and began to cool off in 1865. A few notes about those times will indicate the extent and nature of that excitement. The Bulletin was the principal journal of the day to shout 'Halt,' and try to stem the current."

"San Francisco was oil mad with the rest of the state, and large companies were formed there and elsewhere in the state. Many, especially from Southern California, were exploited in the East. For instance, we learn from the Philadelphia Railroad and Mining Register of December 3, 1864, as follows:

"California oil land shares, subscribed for in this city at $1,000 per share, advanced $500 per share in gold two days after the subscription list was filled. These oil lands are in the Los Angeles district, in the southern portion of California. A letter describing these lands says: 'The rancheros have always looked upon them as objectionable on account of their losing many cattle by their becoming mired in the oil that overflows hundreds of acres around the mouths of the wells.'"

"It may be cruel to certain struggling promoters of today to rake that out of a dead past, but some people would be better for a few groans. So let them have this brief tale of the California petroleum; Its flaming prospectus announced its capital at $10,000,000. Its property was a Spanish grant in Santa Barbara county, stated to consist of 10,000 acres. Some fellow bought it for $22,000 in greenbacks, or about $10,000 in gold. The deal was telegraphed to Eastern associates, who sold one-half for $50,-000. Then it sold for $450,000, and then it went into the assets of the California Petroleum Company at $10,000,000. In their wonderful prospectus the Eastern boomers told of "twenty natural oil wells of the largest size" on the land. In a big advertisement in the New York Independent, it was stated "that the spring marked No. 1 on the map" was estimated to contain 144,500,000 gallons of oil, "actually in sight." If only ten successful wells were developed the yield in twelve months would be of the value of $5,460,000, while the company had actually twenty flowing wells. One-tenth of the capital stock was reserved as a working capital, and one-half of this was offered at $35 per share, par value being $100.

New York correspondence tells that "Professor J. T. Hodges, with a full corps of assistants, machinery, etc., is to leave New York soon for the California oil fields. The company expects to place cargoes of oil in New York in a few months." Many companies, with millions of capital stock were exploited in the East and vast tracts were bought or bonded. All over the state the smallest seepages indicating oil precipitated rushes. Napa county joined in the excitement, and in the Napa Reporter of March 25, we find: "Last week a hired man who was excited over the reports of oil discoveries in other parts of the State was seen digging in a swamp for some purpose not stated. In a short time he cried out; 'I've struck it, I've struck it,' and dropped to the ground with his head over the newly made hole. On Mr. Goodrich approaching, much amazed he was told. 'Here is an oil spring, smell the oil,' holding up a handful of the fresh mud, whose strong kerosene odor was unmistakable evidence. Measures have been taken for the immediate incorporation of a petroleum company, with a capital stock of $600,000. Parties from one end of the valley to the other are searching for oil."

All the New York papers glowed with accounts of the wonderful California oil discoveries, and the State local papers had plenty of oil news and confidence. A common item was: "The rush to the oil regions continues." The Fresno Times of Millerton put it: "Our last advices from the oil region of this county are very encouraging. The excitement remains at fever heat."

Alas, they ran all over the Coalinga district too. A previous item in the Fresno Times says: "Oil wells have lately been discovered on the eastern slope of the Coast Range in Fresno county, near Vallecito Canyon, and about two miles south of the ranch of Griswold and Anderson. Frank Dusy and John Clark of Bear Valley are the original discoverers of the oil springs in

Fresno, and each of them has secured 160 acres, under the act regulating possessory claims. These claims were taken up December 21, 1864." The exact location of these original claims is unknown to the writer, but the story is interesting in view of what happened on the eastern slope of Fresno county thirty odd years later. That oil had to wait all that time for Chanslor and Canfield who were probably innocent little cherubs somewhere and had never smelled kerosene or dreamed of a Blue Goose strike that fate had put away on the shelf for them. There ought to be a "Dusy" and "John Clark" well down there somewhere in honor of the pioneer prospectors of the Fresno oil fields.

The Bulletin of March 25, 1864, tells that "a company has just begun operations on a mountain of sand and petroleum in Santa Cruz county." Operations were numerous in all the coast and valley counties. A Humboldt correspondent writes: "Humboldt county is destined to be one of the greatest oil-producing regions in the world." Maybe it is. Early in 1865 seventeen wells were going down in the Matthole district in Humboldt county, and the Irwin Davis well was down 310 feet. A few months ago rushers were again locating hundreds of claims in that district and wells are going down again as elsewhere in that northern coast region.

"The oil country is still full of people locating claims," said the Marysville Appeal in April, 1865, referring to Colusa county, where operators are now putting down prospect wells. In Contra Costa county the Seaver farm of 200 acres on San Pablo Creek, sold in 1865 for $10,800 to an oil company, and many similar investments were made in the Mt. Diablo region. Many shafts and wells were sunk short distances.

The San Mateo Gazette of April, 1865, describes the oil future of that county with the evidence of the real thing before it to justify the prediction. It said: "San Mateo county will make as good if not better show of coal oil than any other county in the State. We have some samples of rock in our office from the bed of the Purissima Creek, near B. G. Lathrope's sulphur springs that are so completely saturated with coal oil that it will burn almost equal to a kerosene lamp. With such evidence, why may we not rival creeks in Pensylvania."

What is now the "Sunset" field in Kern county drew one of the rushes. It was long years before oil was produced there, and then on a small scale, until the deeper wells of a few months ago revealed for the first time the bituminous wealth near Buena Vista Lake. As it happened there and in Fresno county, oil in paying quantitities will undoubtedly be found in many fields fruitlessly exploited in the sixties and again during that second oil boom in the seventies. These few glimpses at the earliest oil boom are not discouraging evidence for enterprising and intelligent oil operators of today who have experience, judgment and knowledge possessed by nobody then.

SOME ANCIENT HISTORY.

The following account of early oil history in California is from the veracious pen of "Bill, the Bos'un," the able writer of ancient history in the Los Angeles Sunday Times.

"The first discoveries of petroleum in this State were made in Humboldt county in 1863 and the place was at once called Petrolia, for advertising purposes. Small lots were shipped down to San Francisco from that place, and the shippers represented the supply as inexhaustible. Capt. James Whitney, then president of the California Steam Navigation Company, was persuaded to make a trial of it on account of its cheapness; and had the low-pressure steamboat Amelia (afterwards owned by the Banning Bros., in the Catalina Island trade) altered in her furnaces so as to burn the stuff. A trial trip was made in May, 1866, and every prominent stockholder in the company was aboard for a voyage around Mare Island. Whether it was that they did not know how to handle the oil, or what was really the matter at all, I do not know, but I do know that there were several millionaires on board of her that were glad to get ashore alive, for she caught fire four times inside of three hours. Now there are a dozen steamers using petroleum for fuel and none of them have caught fire in the last seven years to my knowledge. Whether it was through jealousy of San Francisco or what other cause, I cannot say, but Sacramento went in strong on speculation in Humboldt petroleum lands and stocks, while San Francisco 'wouldn't have it' at any price. The consequence was that some citizens of the capital city lost a good deal of money in wells that failed to flow. Not one of them ever dreamed of such a thing then as petroleum in Southern California, which was credited at that time with no other products than fat beef and Angelica wine. How things have changed, by the way."

It is interesting to note that most of the successful oil fields of the State are on the site of early explorations, which proved unprofitable to the men who tried, thirty years too soon, to open up the oil industry. In the history of the oil production by counties will be found an account of the early work in the various fields. But a brief account of some of the work in other days cannot fail to be of interest. As early as 1857 a coast trading schooner took a barrel of Ventura county oil to San Francisco. It had been obtained by bailing out of a shallow hole blasted in the rock. There was a difference of opinion in San Francisco as to the oil. Some said it was oil of tar, while others claimed that it was similar to the Pennsylvania product.

But although the wiseacres of the coast failed to realize and appropriate the riches lying under their feet, eastern capital was more easily interested. Numerous purchases were made of land in what is now Ventura county, the investment being backed by Tom Scott, the coal and iron king of Pennsylvania. Throughout the State from San Diego in the South to Colusa in the north, every one was talking oil and there were thousands of prospective millionaires, who indignantly refused offers for their land, which would have been considered preposterous a few years earlier. Even at that early date a claim was filed in the ocean near Santa Barbara where, since then, a number of wharves have been built and much oil pumped out. Such capitalists as Stanford, Hayward, Coleman, Senators Jones and Hearst, D. O. Mills, and Haggin and Tevis all had investments in oil lands. When it was found that instead of the estimates of thousands of barrels to the well in twenty-four hours the wells yielded only from one to five barrels a day, and that of a thick oil containing but a small proportion of illuminant, the excitement rapidly subsided. It remained for another generation to learn the secret of the oil values of the state. In reviewing all of the early failures and disappointments, in the light of the knowledge of this the year of our Lord 1900, it is not out of place to observe, "Verily, the stone which the builders rejected is become the head of the corner."

Graham, Photographer.

OIL SEEPAGE, VENTURA COUNTY. A GREAT STREAM OF OIL PARTIALLY SUBMERGES LOGS AS SHOWN IN CUT.

GEOLOGICAL

By Prof. W. L. Watts, Assistant in Field, California State Mining Bureau.

CALIFORNIA'S mineral wealth consists not only in those minerals from which metals are obtained, but also in numerous mineral substances which become greater in demand as our manufacturing interests expand, and as our civilization advances.

The most important of the latter class of minerals, which, in a commercial sense, may be regarded as non-metallic, are the hydrocarbons; and of these, petroleum, in the form of asphaltum and oil and natural gas, is of the greatest value. This paper is confined to the last two of these items.

In California, the question of petroleum as fuel assumes a special importance, owing to the fact that the deposits of coal, which have thus far been discovered in our State, are inadequate to the steadily increasing demand for fuel.

The object of this paper is to summarize the leading facts concerning the occurrence of petroleum in California. This mineral, in the form of natural gas, oil and asphaltum, is found at various places in the Coast Range. The greatest showing of petroleum, and the greatest development of the petroleum industry are south of San Francisco. Oil and gas are found in the foothills of the Sierras, and natural gas is obtained in valuable quantities from wells drilled in the great central valley of California. It is said that this gas has also been observed in other counties including the foothills of the Sierras.

The geological formations yielding petroleum in California range from the lower cretaceous to the quaternary; and, in different localities, the geological horizon of the productive strata differs in point of vertical range. In the Puente Hills, and at Los Angeles, the oil-yielding rocks are of Noecene age; these formations were first classed as Pliocene, on account of the numerous Pliocene fossils found in them.

On the south side of the valley of the Santa Clara River, in Ventura and Los Angeles counties, the principal oil-yielding formations probably range from the Neocene to the Miocene. The writer has not yet made a detailed examination of these oil fields:

On the north side of the valley of the Santa Clara River, in Ventura county, there is evidence of petroleum in rocks ranging from the upper Neocene to the lower Eocene formations; the productive formation ranging from the Miocene to the uppermost portion of the Eocene.

In the foothills west of Bakersfield, in Kern county, petroleum is found in formations ranging from the Eocene to the Neocene, and heretofore classed as Pliocene; but the oil-yielding formations, which have been tested by drilling, are supposed to be of Miocene age.

Natural gas and oil have also been obtained in the foothills of the Sierras, east of Bakersfield, the formation being either of Pliocene or of Neocene age.

In Fresno county and Kings county there are exudations of petroleum from rocks of Miocene age; but the petroleum yielding formation near Coalinga, in Fresno county, which has recently proved very remunerative, appear to be of Eocene age, formerly called Cretaceous B.

The geological horizon of the oil-yielding rocks at Moody Gulch, Santa Clara county, has never been determined.

Some oil has also been obtained on the Tunitas and the Purissima creeks, in San Mateo county, from wells which penetrate strata which are, probably, of Eocene age.

North of San Francisco, petroleum-yielding formations crop out along the coast at Bolinas Bay and at Point Arena; at these places the exposed rocks are either of Pliocene or of Neocene age.

In Humboldt county, several wells have been drilled, from which some oil has been obtained, the rocks penetrated being either of Pliocene or of Neocene age.

On Bear Creek, in Colusa county, gas and oil are found in rocks of cretaceous age.

It is reported that in some places petroleum is found permeating eruptive or other crystalline rocks.

At Stockton, in San Joaquin county, natural gas is obtained in remunerative quantities, from wells permeating strata of quaternary age.

At Marysville Buttes, in the Sacramento Valley, natural gas is found in rocks of Eocene age, formerly called Cretaceous B. There are several places in Sacramento and San Joaquin valleys where wells are yielding suffiicient natural gas to be of local value.

The relative position in point of verticle range of the formations, wherein remunerative oil wells have been obtained, in Ventura and Los Angeles counties, is demonstrated by an investigation of the country between the Piru and Sespe creeks, in Ventura county and the following sequence of formations can be seen: At the Piru creek, a conglomerate formation is seen containing Neocene fossils, Pliocene formations being the most numerous. In some places the conglomerate is impregnated with petroleum; it rests on a shale formation, containing Neocene fossils. The lower portion of the shale is interstratified with sandstone, which, in many places, is impregnated with petroleum, forming an oil sand, the outcropping strata of which resemble the oil sands seen in the Puente hills, in Los Angeles county. The shale rests on a whitish sandstone of Miocene age. This whitish sandstone contains remunerative oil-yielding strata.

The conglomerate, the shale, and the whitish sandstone in Ventura county constitute a group corresponding to a group of certain conglomerates, shales, and sandstones which the writer carefully studied in the Puente hills, in Los Angeles county. These formations probably form a large portion of the rocks in the oil districts of Los Angeles and Ventura counties; and, in both of these counties, these formations are of similar character and contain formations of similar age.

As observed in the Puente hills, in Los Angeles county, these whitish sandstones, shales and conglomerates rest on one another in the order here named. The principal oil-yielding formations found in these hills, and in the city of Los Angeles, are certain oil sands which interstratify the lower portion of the shale formation, and, probably constitute the uppermost strata of the underlying sandstones.

The whitish sandstone formation extends westward from the Piru Creek, in Ventura county, to the Sespe oil district, also in Ventura county, the distance between the two places being about eight miles.

At the Sespe oil district, the whitish sandstone rests on a shale formation, whitish and grayish at the top but passing into a dark-colored shale which is interbedded with numerous thin strata, or nodular masses of hard bituminous limestone. These shales contain Miocene and Eocene fossils, and rest on a drab-colored sandstone, of no great thickness. The drab-colored sandstone rests on a brown sandstone, locally known as the Sespe brown stone. This brown stone rests on white sandstone, and the latter on a buff-colored sandstone. The Sespe brown stone, the white sandstone, and the buff-colored sandstone all contain typical Eocene fossils. All these sandstones are more or less imbedded with shale. The principal oil-yielding formations in the Sespe district are the lowermost portion of the dark-colored shales, the drab sandstone, and the uppermost portion of the Sespe brown stone.

There are numerous seepages of petroleum in the hard, buff-colored Eocene sandstones; but no remunerative oil wells have as yet been obtained by drilling in these rocks.

Between the Piru Creek and the Sespe district no marked non-conformity was observed by the writer, the variations of the dip being referable rather to local geological disturbance than to non-conformability. Still, it by no means follows that the formations actually rest comformably on one another. It is generally believed that in California the Miocene formations rest non-conformably on the Eocene. Observations in Los Angeles and Orange counties lead to the conclusion that the Neocene shales overlap the whitish sandstones; and there are some reasons for believing that the conglomerate rests non-conformably on the Neocene shales.

Since the Neocene period there have been not only epochs of unusual geologic disturbance, but also disturbance of a chronic nature which has been cotemporaneous with the disposition of the tertiary and quaternary formaations. Similar disturbances continue to this day. It appears that in many instances these disturbances were of local character.

The formations penetrated by remunerative oil wells, in such portions of Los Angeles, Orange and Ventura counties as have been examined by the writer are as follows:

In the territory extending between the Santa Ana River, in Orange county, and the ocean, at Santa Monica, in Los Angeles county, remunerative oil sands have been found in the lower portion of the Neocene shales, and probably in the upper portion of the Miocene sandstone. In one instance oil was found in the overlying conglomerate.

At the Modello oil wells, near Piru, in Ventura county, remunerative oil sands have been found in the whitish sandstones of the Miocene age.

In the Sespe district remunerative oil sands have been found in the upper portion of the Eocene sandstones and in shales, which appear to occupy a position between the Miocene and Eocene formations.

It is probable that these oil-yielding localities have their counterpart in many other places in California besides those which have been mentioned, for the geological formations constituting these oil measures extend along the Coast Range from San Diego county to Humboldt county. We have not yet obtained sufficient geological evidence to warrant the expression of anything more than a tentative opinion concerning the actual geological horizon of the petroleum formations in the following oil fields: The oil fields on the south side of the Santa Clara river, those north of Santa Paula, in Ventura county, and those of Santa Barbara, Kern, Santa Clara and San Mateo counties. But the data already accumulated warrant the assertion that the oil measures, in the localities referred to, are of tertiary age.

From the description of the oil yielding formations, the geological position of which has been definitely determined, it appears, that the productive strata are sandstones, underlying or interstratifying bodies of shale. It may be argued that these conditions indicate natural distillation as the chief cause of the accumulation of petroleum in the oil measures.

In many parts of California we find petroleum-yielding formations associated with shales, which show signs of having been subjected to metamorphic action. It is reasonable to infer that the petroleum, having been elaborated in the shale, may have been driven out of it by natural distillation into inclosing or interstratifying beds of sandstone.

It must also be borne in mind that, in other instances, petroleum may have been collected, by upward distillation, from sedimentary strata underlying the shale.

A very small percentage of petroleu m originally distributed through a great thickness of strata, might be driven into different zones by natural distillation; and, at certain temperature and pressure, it would pass readily through sandstone. The upward course of the petroleum might be impeded by strata of shale, and, when the temperature decreased, the petroleum might condense in any rocks sufficiently porous to afford it storage. If the shale were only partially impervious to the petroleum the former would be, more or less, permeated by the latter, and fractures in the shale would give the petroleum access to overlying formations.

A modification of such processes, by gas or hydrostatic pressure, would be quite sufficient to bring about a redistribution of the petroleum, and the formation of secondary deposits of that mineral.

The oil-yielding formations of California, in common with the other rocks of the Coast Range, show great geological disturbance; and the complex structure resulting therefrom has given rise to somewhat difficult geological problems in regard to the oil fields of this State.

In a general way, it may be said that the oil lines, or lines along which remunerative wells may be found, follow the strike of the axes of folds in the rocks, or the course of faults which have isolated blocks of strata inclosing the oil-yielding rocks. The tracing of oil lines in this State and the development of oil fields, necessitates a competent knowledge of structural geology, without which the risks of oil mining would be greatly increased.

The depth of oil wells depends on the angle at which the oil sand dips, and the distance the wells are from the outcrop of the oil sand, or from the axis of the fold on which the wells are situated.

As a general statement, it may be said that the most productive wells are about 1000 feet in depth, some being much deeper.

The "life" and yield of such wells are naturally varied. In some instances, they "started off" with a yield of 100 barrels, or more, a day; but, in the course of five or six years, the yield diminished to ten barrels or less a day. In other instances, the first yield was less than 100 barrels a day, but the rate of the production was better sustained during the "life" of the well.

Points on Prospecting for Petroleum

[From "The Genesis of Petroleum and Asphaltum in California," by A. S. Cooper, State Mineralogist.]

SURFACE indications of the presence of petroleum consist of unaltered rocks, white-leached shales, and sandstones, shales burnt to redness, fumaroles, mineral springs and the residue from mineral springs, such as selenite, etc., subsidences, natural gas, springs of petroleum oil and maltha, porous rocks saturated with bitumen, cracks in shale and other rocks filled or partly filled with bitumen, black silicified shales.

It would seem like supererogation to say that petroleum oil is not found in any notable quantity in metamorphic rocks, and if found at all that it is a secondary deposit. One may as well expect to find accumulations of petroleum in a limekiln as in metamorphic rocks, yet notwithstanding this fact, which one would think would be patent to every person, wells for oil have been drilled in granite. The prospector should confine his attention to the unaltered rocks.

The color of the bitumens, when they exist near the surface of the earth, is black, bluish black, and brownand dirty brown. The bitumen can be determined from coal, vegetable deposits, iron, manganese, and other minerals that closely resemble it, by the following tests: By its bituminous odor and taste; by melting in the flame of a match or candle with a bituminous odor (iron and manganese do not fuse, and coal and vegetable matter burn without fusion;) by dissolving in bisulphide of carbon, chloroform, and turpentine.

It would be well in prospecting for oil, to carry a small bottle of one of these solvents and another small bottle in which the substance to be determined is placed in a comminuted form and agitated. If a brown or black solution is formed, the substance under examination is bitumen. Iron, manganese, coal and vegetable matter do not dissolve in these solvents.

All streams, pools and other bodies of water should be carefully inspected. If oil is present it will float on the surface, showing prismatic colors. Compounds of iron floating on the surface of water frequently show these iridescent colors. Whether this scum is oil or an iron compound can be determined by stirring the surface of the water with a circular motion. If iron, the scum will break into irregular fragments, and if oil it will form bands of color. In other words, the iron compound seems to act and break like a solid, whereas the oily scum acts like a liquid.

Frequently gases are seen to ascend from the bottom of streams and pools of water. In the bed of La Brea Creek, upon the Sisquoc Rancho, Santa Barbara county, gases rise from the bottom of the creek for a distance exceeding one mile, which can be lit upon the surface of the water and burn with a luminous flame. This occurs in many other places in California.

Carburetted hydrogen, or natural gas, is a far greater indication of the presence of the bitumens than is sulphurreted hydrogen or carbonic acid gas; consequently it is frequently important to determine between these gases. Carburreted hydrogen burns with a yellow, luminous flame, where-

A RIVER OF OIL ON THE BARD RANCH, VENTURA COUNTY

Graham, Photographer.

as sulphurreted hydrogen burns with a bluish flame. A familiar example of the color of these flames is shown in the burning of an ordinary match. Light the match, and while the sulphured end is burning a bluish flame is shown. When the sulphur is consumed and the wood alone burns, a luminous flame is shown. Sulphurreted hydrogen has a strong odor of sulphur, and when a brightened piece of silver is held in it the silver becomes blackened. Carbonic acid gas does not burn.

If carburetted hydrogen is found it is nearly a certain sign that somewhere in the formation liquid bitumens exist, although they may be distant from the place where the gas issues.

All outcrops of the stratified rocks should be examined. There are generally better exposures of these rocks on the sides of streams, canyons and gulches than elsewhere. The surface of the ground should also be examined. If any brown or black material is seen in the seams of the rocks or saturated porous strata, the test for bitumens with solvents as described herein should be made.

If natural gas or bitumen is found upon the surface of shale there is a strong probability that the bitumen has ascended vertically through these rocks from porous strata below, as the avenues for the migration of the bitumen are usually seams and cracks in the shale, the shale itself being impervious to the flow of the bitumens especially the liquid ones. But when porous sand is reached, or when the outcrop is porous sand, it can be presumed that the bitumens reached the surface through the sand. Especially is this liable to be true if the sandstones stand at a high angle with the horizon.

Subsidences are indicative of the presence of petroleum, but if any oil is found in them it will be viscous and heavy, the fractured condition of the earth in the subsidence permitting the escape of the volatile parts of the oil. This is also true of the burned shales, if any petroleum exists in these shales it would be a secondary deposit, having entered the shales after they were burned. Petroleum vapor in all probability assisted in the burning of these shales.

As mineral waters always accompany the bitumens, mineral springs and the evidences of former mineral springs are to a limited extent evidence of the accumulations of bitumens. Selenite, travertine, infusorial earth, and a number of other mineral deposits are evidences of former mineral springs. When bitumens exist in a formation they are more often than otherwise overlaid with white leached shales and sandstones; therefore, these rocks are an indication of the bitumens to a certain extent, and, owing to their conspicuous color, can be seen from a long distance.

Therefore, outcrops and anticlines can be followed from outside property into the property being examined, and the structure be considered sufficiently well demonstrated so as to justify a person in drilling a well for oil, even if bitumens were absent from the surface of the land upon which the well is to be drilled and the exposures of the strata are but slight. The strike of the anticlines and outcrops can be determined by a pocket compass.

If indications of the presence of bitumens are sufficient to justify it, a topographical map of the presumed oil territory should be made before making a cross-section of the rock structure. If a person is incapable of making a topographical map of the territory, he certainly has not the capacity of making sectional views of the same showing the structure, the latter operation being much more difficult and largely dependent upon the former.

All indications should be closely examined and thoroughly studied. Even with the greatest attention given to these details before selecting a place to drill a well, there is danger that the lower parts of the bituminous strata encountered in the well may contain water in place of gas and oil; or may be calcified or silicified instead of being bituminized; or that water has entered the outcrop of the strata at higher altitudes and ascended through the formation, floating the oil to the surface or carrying the same to the other dip of the anticline.

Theory and observations cannot be perfect but are far better than guessing.

Clairvoyants can see as far into a millstone as anyone, but no farther. Divining rods were first used to detect perjurers, but since liars have commenced to use them they have lost their virtue and are of no value. Accumulations of fossil shells and bones are not indices to deposits of bitumen; vast masses of shells and bones exist where there is no petroleum. The same compass bearing is not applicable to all deposits of oil. Hardly any two have the same strike, and the strike is frequently curved. The age of the unaltered rocks bears no relation to the accumulations of bitumen.

The mere geological age of the unaltered shales and sandstones in California does not inform us of the nature of these rocks; nor can we, on the other hand, from their petrographic character, arrive at the geological age of these rocks. No kind of unaltered shale or sandstone is restricted to any particular period.

Some California Geology

[From "The Genesis of Petroleum and Asphaltum in California," by A. S. Cooper, State Mineralogist.]

ANTICLINES, synclines, monoclines, centroclines, and quaquaversals, and also faults, exert a great influence in the accumulation of gas, petroleum oil, and water. Especially is this true in California, where the dips and undulations along the strike of the anticline are exposed and well defined.

Although a description of the different inclinations and curvatures of strata would seem elemental, a thorough knowledge of the effect of these inclinations is necessary for an understanding of the laws governing the accumulations of bitumen in California. In the Eastern states the slopes of the domes frequently do not exceed twenty feet to a mile, whereas in California the strata stand at a very steep angle with the horizon, frequently being overturned.

When a group of strata is bent into a curve like a saddle, with its convexity towards the earth, it is called an anticlinal curve. A synclinal curve is exactly the opposite of an anticlinal curve. When the strata are folded or curved, so as to form a trough, the concave side of which is turned from the earth, this is called a synclinal curve. In both anticlines and synclines, the line in each bed, along which the change in the direction of the dip takes place, is called the anticlinal or synclinal axis of that bed, and the planes containing all the axes of an anticlinal ridge, or a synclinal trough, are called axis planes. The axis plane usually approaches verticality. Anticlines and synclines frequently nose out, or coalesce.

When an anticline undulates along the line of its axis, dome-like elevations occur, from the summits of which the beds dip away in every direction. In this case the strata are said to have a quaquaversal dip. An anticline is an elongated dome.

A quaquaversal, or dome, is a nest, usually of a great number, of different strata composing numerous overlying, gigantic, inverted funnels, the strata of the formation forming the sides of these rock funnels, all of which tend to guide and convey the ascending gas and oil to the apex of the dome.

When a syncline undulates along the line of its axis, basin-shaped detions occur, from the summits of which the beds dip from all sides. This is called a centroclinal dip. A syncline is an elongated basin.

A fault, or dislocation, is a fissure or crack in the crust of the earth, accompanied by the elevation of the mass upon one side of the fault, while the other side remains stationary, or sinks down. Anticlines and synclines are often truncated by faults, and may be so faulted as to form the segments of a sphere or cone. If an oil-bearing bed, ascending to the north, be interrupted by an east and west fault, the further ascent of the oil northwards will be arrested, and then an abundant supply of oil may be obtained by boring on the south side of the fault; while for a considerable distance to the north, water will occupy the formation, to the exclusion of the oil. This is more apt to be the case where the throw of the fault is sufficient so that the edges of the porous strata are covered by impervious strata. Selvage frequently occupies the line of faults, generally caused by the movement of the two sides of the fault on each other, which have ground up the materials of the rock, forming a sheet of matter impervious to the flow of oil or water, or the faults may be filled up with mineral matter of various kinds, which are also impervious to oil or water.

When a formation contains permanent water, the accumulation of petroleum oil will be found near the upper part of the dome. The oil floats on the surface of the water, and if natural gas is present, it will be found above the oil. These three substances arrange themselves according to their specific gravity, the lightest on top.

The unaltered rocks of California cover an area of forty thousand square miles.

The bitumens are found, in greater or less quantities, in all of the unaltered rocks of California of the cretaceous and tertiary periods, and sometimes in the quarternary rocks, in the form of natural gas, petroleum oil, and solid and liquid asphaltum. The difficulty is the discovery of accumulations at particular places large enough to justify developments.

The unaltered rocks consist principally of alternating beds of shale, sandstone, and conglomerate, varying in thickness and resting upon metamorphic rock. The sandstones and conglomerates act as reservoirs for the accumulations of bitumen, and the shales as incasements for these reservoirs. Some of these sandstone beds are more than three hundred feet in thickness as will be described hereafter.

Anticlines exercise great influence upon the accumulation of natural petroleum oil and other bitumens.

The main anticlines of California oil regions bear northwesterly and southeasterly. The summits of these anticlines have been denuded, exposing metamorphic rock. Numerous smaller anticlines branch in all directions from these main anticlines, and generally nose out in the valleys.

Smaller and lower anticlines also run rudely parallel with the main anticlines.

When the uplifts, by orogenic movements, have been great, the apexes of the anticlines are frequently denuded, the bitumens being either washed away or, as more often happens, drained into the dips of the anticlines.

The petroleum-bearing strata are exposed to a greater geological depth in the outcrops of the strata of the main anticlines that show a metamorphic core, than in the lower anticlines that are but slightly denuded; consequently there are visible many seepages of oil and flows of gas from the outcrops of oil strata on the sides of the main anticlines, while in the lower anticlines the same oil strata lie far below the surface of the earth. In the valleys in which bitumous strata are overlaid by quarternary rocks, the bituminous deposits may exist at such great depths that they cannot be reached by drilling.

In the northern part of the state a large amount of tertiary rocks have been washed away; these rocks grow thicker and thicker to the south ward until in the southern part of the state they are of great thickness. The unaltered rocks in the northern part of the state are geographically higher and more broken than in the southern part. Owing to these different conditions, there is more and better storage room for the bitumens in the southern part of the state than in the northern part of the state.

The unaltered rocks of the Coast Range are more broken and contorted, and have a much larger outcrop than those forming the foothills of the Sierra Nevada on the east side of San Joaquin valley. Therefore, there are more visible evidences of bitumen on the west side than on the east side of the valley.

There can be no question but that the cretaceous and tertiary rocks, which are the oil-bearing rocks of California, underlie the quaternary deposits of San Joaquin and Sacramento valleys. Gas wells exist in these valleys; this shows that the lighter and more volatile parts of the petroleum oil have been preserved; consequently, the heavier parts of the oil exist.

OIL PRODUCTION IN CALIFORNIA BY YEARS.

	Barrels.
Previous to 1876 (estimated)	175,000
1876	12,000
1877	13,000
1878	15,227
1879	19,858
1880	40,552
1881	99,862
1882	128,636
1883	142,857
1884	262,000
1885	325,000
1886	377,145
1887	678,572
1888	690,333
1889	303,220
1890	307,360
1891	323,600
1892	385,049
1893	470,179
1894	705,969
1895	1,208,482
1896	1,252,777
1897	1,903,411
1898	2,257,207
1899	2,292,123
Total	14,389,379

WHERE OIL WAS FIRST FOUND IN LOS ANGELES CITY.

Graham, Photographer.

The Present and Future of Petroleum in California

TO write an accurate summary of the oil situation in California is a task no one dare undertake unless he be endowed with omniscient power. The present situation alone is prospective and problematical. No producing field has yet been thoroughly tested. No man, even if he has traveled from San Diego to Mt. Shasta, even though he be an oil expert beyond compare, can give a decisive and and positive opinion of the present status of the oil situation in California. The situation is complex and diversified. No two districts furnish identically the same conditions. Each field has its local peculiarities. A driller, who is thoruoghly familiar with one district, may be compelled to learn his lessons over again in an adjoining county. Experienced operators from eastern fields are frank to confess their inability to cope with local conditions without first making a study of local geography. This statement of conditions being admitted, it is not to be wondered at that scientific men have many times been mistaken regarding the oil indications and that practical drillers have spent large sums in sinking dry holes.

And if the present is a problem, how much more difficult is it to prognosticate the future? Difficulties there are of course, but American genius and pluck and energy has surmounted difficulties many times as hard. It is not true that the industry is merely speculative. At least, it is no more speculative than raising oranges, which depend for success upon soil, moisture and climatic conditions; not more speculative than any branch of mercantile trade; certainly not more speculative than honest mining. Pick and shovel and giant powder, when wisely and honestly applied, will in the end bring sure reward; derrick and drill, when intelligently put to work on an oil strike is certain to produce the same happy result.

It is true that there are some persons in California who are making oil a gambling device. It is true that when you mention the word oil to a person, he is very apt to throw to the winds every business principle on which he has acted through his whole life. There is something about the oil business which prompts men to dream dreams at the expense of the most common of common sense. They want to get something for nothing and to get it in defiance of every law of industry. But aside from these people, there are not lacking those who realize that if they are to make money out of oil they must adhere to business methods, the first of which is to try to learn something about the business before they embark.

In every district in California there are those who are chasing phantoms and there are those who are working on ordinary business lines, and there is probably no other field of activity in the state at present where the returns to the level-headed man are more apparent or where the prospect for gains in the future are brighter than in oil.

To give an idea of this past and present of the oil industry in California in concise form, this book has been issued. It does not claim to be a complete account either historically, geologically or financially. To do that would require many large octavo volumes. What is here set down is fact so far as the publishers have been able to obtain facts. Few deductions have been attempted. The figures presented show for themselves. What the future has in store for California oil prospectors only the drill can determine. To the student of oil conditions, the publisher can only say, read the record of the past and the account of active work in many fields at present and judge for yourself what the future holds in store.

No better summarized account of the conditions of the oil fields of California can be obtained than from an article in the Los Angeles Herald, written by Edgar F. Howe, than whom there is no more accurate, painstaking and faithful student of the oil industry in the state. Mr. Howe was raised in the heart of the oil bearing section of Pennsylvania, and is thoroughly posted in regard to the oil situation in general. Since coming to California he has made a careful study of the problem of oil in all its details, and his article is from one who tells of what he knows. The article from which the subjoined extracts are made was written after a tour of more than 2,000 miles in which Mr. Howe visited and made a careful study of every oil-producing district of the state.

THE OIL FIELD

Beginning down in Mexico at some unlocated point there is a bitumous belt which extends along the entire Pacific coast as far north as Alaska. In some places this is manifest in the form of coal and in others as gas or oil. It is true that in many localities there is neither oil nor coal in considerable quantities in evidence, but the formation in which bitumens are found is continuous, and the absence of oil is due to the fact that there was no provision for its retention in the rocks.

This belt enters California in San Diego county, passes by Elsinore, Riverside, Fullerton and Los Angeles, whence it reaches the various ranges of hills and mountains which bear the collective title of the coast range, though many of the ranges have independent designations. These mountains are very generally formed into five or six parallel ranges, and extend far beyond the northern confines of the state. The careless observer may not have noted that these ranges are entirely dissimilar to the Sierra Nevadas. The latter are of granitic build, while the coast mountains and hills are devoid of granite, being composed of shale, sandstone and fossiliferous conglomerate, the three principal factors in oil bearing formations everywhere in the world.

As there must be natural reservoirs, in the form of sandstone overlaid with shale, it is evident that oil could not be expected to be present in all places where the formation is favorable, and thus it is that the great belt reaching through the state is not uniformly rich in oil, which is found only in small belts or pools.

Moreover, oil tends naturally to rise to the surface, as it is always under greater or less gas pressure in the rocks, and it is very possible that where the most evidence of oil is found on the surface the least will be found in the ground, though experience in California has shown that this is not the rule to be depended on. It is simply a factor which enters into the problem of locating oil.

The oil belt of California is thus of immense proportions. It is believed to be richest in the southern portion of the state, where the conditions for impounding the oil in sandstone are most abundant. But it is by no means certain that great fields will not be found far to the north.

Taking San Francisco as about the northern end of the field of present activity, the belt has a length of about 600 miles and an average width of about 70 miles, giving an area of 42,000 square miles, or about 27,000,000 acres, in which the formation is favorable for the finding of oil.

Of course no person can tell what portion of this land will be found to really contain oil, but it is evident that even a small percentage of it is sufficient to make California the leading oil producing portion of the country.

Petroleum has so long been used almost exclusively for illuminating purposes that it is not strange that many people forget that it is susceptible to use in other ways. In fact as a fuel it is questionable whether oil has not a greater industrial value on this coast than as an illuminant. It has long been known that oil can be used for fuel purposes, but based on relative prices in the east it has been found that coal is a cheaper fuel than oil. In California, however, the conditions are reversed. Here coal has always been very expensive, and it is shown that on a theoretical basis, oil at $1 per barrel is equivalent to coal at $4.50 per ton, while the cost of coal here is about $7.50 per ton. Oil is therefore about as cheap a fuel in California as any state in the Union has for manufacturing purposes.

But while California has been producing petroleum for two decades, it was not until recently that the supply was great enough to give to manufacturers and railroads any assurance that they would have a steady supply of the fuel, and comparatively few of them were disposed to make use of it. Now, however, with the production climbing up to a point which gives a bountiful supply of oil and an assurance of a steady supply, scores of factories and railroads are resorting to it for fuel, and the very increase in production thus tends to stimulate the supply, there being less of a threat of over-production now than when but a fraction of the present output existed.

OIL FOR REFINING

But while the use of oil as fuel is probably the greatest gain to the state from the new industry, it is not the only one. Here, as elsewhere, oil is being refined for illuminating use, and there is a probability of still greater quantities being so used. Unfortunately the details regarding this use of oil are not available. There are three refineries in the state producing illuminating oil, that of the Puente Oil Company at Chino, the Union Oil Company near San Francisco, and the Pacific Coast Oil Company at San Francisco. In each case the refinery manufactures an unknown quantity of illuminating oil, gasoline, etc., while the residuum is used as asphaltum or fuel oil. The illuminating oil is sold in bulk to the Standard Oil Company, and by the latter it is sold through the state to retailers.

There is a great deal of mystery attached to this refining process, the claim often being made that California oils cannot be refined to produce a satisfactory illuminant, and the various refiners, having a satisfactory market through the Standard company, do not give out encouraging information. It does not appear probable that the Standard company would accept all the oil produced by these three refineries if a satisfactory oil was not produced, and one would expect those companies refining the oil to go out of that branch of the business if it was not a success, which they show no inclination to do. In fact, one of the companies for several years sold its output in competition with the Standard company until the present arrangement was made with the latter.

That there is an obstacle presented, however, in the refining of the oil is evident. The California oil contains asphaltum instead of the paraffine which constitutes the base of eastern oils, and it is difficult to entirely dispense with the smoke-making properties of the oil. To just what degree success is achieved in this line cannot be stated, but there is reason to believe that California refined oil is nearer the standard of eastern oil than the refiners themselves would encourage the people in believing.

In refining oil, only the lighter grades are used, that produced in several districts being unfit for use as illuminating oil, while being as valuable as any for fuel purposes.

LUBRICANTS AND ASPHALTUM

Another property which is very valuable in some of the California wells is lubricating oil. This is found in some cases in an almost pure form, while the oil from many wells is susceptible of being manufactured into lubricating oil, and a considerable portion of the output is thus used.

Still another property of the oil is asphaltum, and thousands of tons of this are shipped to the east annually, besides the quantity used in this state. Not only is asphaltum taken from the oil, but it is found in vast bodies on the surface and under the surface of the ground, sometimes covering hundreds of acres and being many feet in thickness. This has been mined in California in various localities for many years. The early Spaniards knew it as brea, and used it for fuel. Later it came into quite general use for paving purposes and shipments to eastern states became heavy. With the growth of the oil industry the work of extracting asphaltum from the oil grew up, and the latest work in this line is using naphtha as a solvent for the transmission of solid asphaltum from the mountain mines of Santa Barbara county across country to the refinery on the coast, when the naphtha is pumped back to the mine and made to take up another load of asphaltum and flow down through the pipe line again.

There are seven or eight refineries in the state devoted to the extraction of asphaltum from oil, of these four or five being in Los Angeles, and the number and capacity of these are constantly increasing.

It is remarkable what a diversity of oil is found in California. This does not simply refer to differences in different districts, for it often happens that there will be a great dissimilarity in oils produced from neighboring wells. In the entire state the oils vary from 8 to over 50 gravity, both extremes being quite rare. Nor is there any apparent rule that can be laid down to govern the gravity of oils which will be found in any district. I must confess that I accepted at one time the doctrine that gravity of oils would be found to rise as one proceeded northward, due to the fact that there the formations are older. Further observation does not warrant the holding of this view without making enough exceptions to practically annul it. It is true that the highest gravity oil has been found in San Mateo county and the next highest in Fresno county, but it is also true that the heaviest oil is that of the Summerland district, while the Los Angeles and Kern River fields, widely separated, produce but little lighter oil, the Fullerton field, the fartherest south of all, producing oil in some wells as light as 34 gravity. There is therefore no rule to be applied, save the very general one that the lightest oil is where it is found.

Taking the various districts from the south up the San Joaquin valley and then up the coast, the gravity, as near as I have been able to ascertain, ranges as follows: Fullerton, 16 to 34; Brea Canyon, 22; Puente, 22 to 38; Whittier, 22; Los Angeles, 12 to 16; Newhall, 16 to over 50, the later being in one well the oil of which is a pale yellow, having been filtered through granite; Sunset, 12 to 16; Kern River, 12 to 16; McKittrick, 20; Oil City (Coalinga) 30 to 40; Kreyenhagen (lubricating), 43; San Mateo county, two wells, over 50; Ventura county, including a number of related districts, 22 to 36; Summerland, 8 to 16. Above the Summerland district there is a large stretch of country with great present activity in development work, but with little or no production as yet.

There has been considerable discussion regarding the presence of paraffine in some California oils. I have met men who have claimed that in wells in which they have worked paraffine accumulated in the same manner as in the Eastern wells, though it was of a different color. It is on such evidence as this that the claim of the existence of the mineral appears to rest exclusively. I have not found any person who claims that an analysis of any oil showed paraffine, and it seems incredible that it would exist and the fact not be established in a scientific manner. I have met other persons who have stated that in drilling wells they have met with a form of earth which acted something like paraffine, clogging the wells like the latter, but which was something entirely different. There does not appear to be any reason to believe that any paraffine has ever been found in a California oil well, nor that anything but oil with an asphaltum base has ever been found.

It has been the experience in the oil industry that whenever a new oil has been found it has taken some time to discover a proper means for refining it, and there does not appear to be any reason to believe that an insurmountable obstacle will be found to be presented in refining the lighter oils of this State.

OUTPUT OF OIL

It is very doubtful whether any person is in a position to give an accurate statement of the output of oil in California, and those who have the most reliable information are not disposed to make it public. Taking the various districts, there is a great diversity of production of the wells, ranging from one barrel per day for some of the Summerland wells to 800 barrels per day for one well in the Oil City (Coalinga) district. There is such a disposition in the various districts to overstate the output of the respective wells that accurate information is very difficult to obtain. Everywhere one hears of wells producing 100 barrels per day, but the phrase seems to be used simply as a convenient expression for carrying the idea that a good well has been found. There are some wells which actually produce 100 barrels per day, and a few that produce considerably more than that amount, but I am inclined to believe that there are not more than a score of such wells in the State. Insomuch as a well producing one barrel per day in some fields pays a good profit and in all fields pays expenses of most wells, it is evident that one can greatly discount the story of 100-barrel wells and yet have a large profit in sight.

The figures are changing rapidly for all the districts in the State, though in some of the districts it is expected that the increase will be vastly greater than in others. But in a territory where the work has been in progress for years and there is a large number of wells, the tendency will be for the new wells to be partially offset by the gradual exhaustion of the old ones experienced in every district, though there is still a prospect of the sinking of the wells to a lower level and the renewal of their lives. But as against this condition in the local field, there is in almost every other field the fact that there is a large body of untouched land. This is even true of the Ventura county fields, where the first wells were sunk about twenty years ago.

In fields near Los Angeles, along the Santa Monica mountains, there is apt to spring up a new field, and this will be practically a continuation of the Los Angeles field.

But in the vast reaches of country along the various branches of the Coast Range there is such an immensity of country that is as yet untouched or only partially prospected that it is to such places one must look for the great fields of the future. These extend all the way from Fullerton beyond Coalinga and San Luis Obispo and through the almost unknown reaches between.

LIFE OF WELLS

A great many people are asking how long the oil wells of California will last. There will be great inequality in this respect, but there is reason to believe that the petroleum industry will be as great a century hence as at present, at least, as the field is such that it will take many years to outline it, while the present individual wells will without question be producing many years from now. The oldest wells in the State are those known as No. 6, in the Ojai Valley, Ventura county, they having been pumped for over twenty years. There are other wells which have dwindled down and become practically valueless in less time, but they have reached but the first oil sand generally, and there is a chance to renew their life by deepening to the second oil sand. In California the deepest wells are but about 1800 feet, while those of Pennsylvania usually range between 2000 and 3000 feet. In the latter State there are wells which have been producing steadily for 35 years, and I am inclined to believe that some of those in California will last even longer, for the reason that the oil sand is deeper and the oil is heavier, thus making its exit from the rock in which it is imprisoned more slowly. There are fields like the Kern River, McKittrick and Whittier, Puente and Fullerton, where the oil sand ranges above 200 feet in thickness generally, and in some cases more than 400 feet. This sand carries from 10 to 15 per cent. of its bulk in oil, and with oils of heavy gravity it will take many years to exhaust the supply. With all the districts, even those so well exploited as Los Angeles, there is practically no knowledge of what lies below the second oil sand, and it is a reasonable belief that fully as great riches are hidden at lower levels, the oil of the lower strata being of lighter gravity, as well as probably more abundant.

COST OF WELLS

There is a wonderful diversity in the cost of wells in the various districts, and even between wells in the same district. The lowest cost is undoubtedly in the Summerland field, where the expense of sinking a well to the first sand, at a depth of about 150 feet, does not exceed $300, including the whole equipment. That explains why in that district it is possible to run a well producing but one barrel of oil per day at a profit, the owner being able to hire it pumped for $10 per month. The most expensive well I have heard of is in the Oil City field, it having cost over $35,000. This well was but 1200 feet deep, but the disintegrate character of the shale encountered, and the consequent disposition of the well to cave in, made it very difficult to get the drill down. In the Los Angeles field the expense of sinking a well usually ranges from $500 to $3000, the expense having been greatly increased by the rise in the price of all kinds of iron work, and particularly of casing, the increase in price of which has exceeded 150 per cent. in a year.

In sinking a well one can never place a close estimate on the cost, as there are so many unseen obstacles presented, and two wells side by side may vary greatly in cost.

Speaking generally, allowing for many exceptions, it can be said that there is compensation for heavy expense in the wells in greater production. As a rule, the shallow wells are not as prolific producers as the deep wells, nor do they turn out as light a gravity of oil. It not infrequently happens, as at Sunset and Summerland, that the oils first produced are very heavy, while by sinking to a greater depth a light oil is obtained.

TOPOGRAPHY AND APPEARANCES

Altitude is not an element in determining the presence of oil, for there are wells under the sea at Summerland and on the mountains in several districts. But altitude above the surrounding country is an element of importance, for while oil is sometimes found in canyons between hills and mountains, here, as in the Eastern fields, it is generally considered that the prospects are best on anticlinal hills. That means on hills drawn out to considerable length, and therein there is the best prospect for finding a reservoir of oil in the rocks. Even in the Summerland field there is a ridge of land projecting into the ocean, and it is in this ridge that the oil is found.

But as for the surface appearance of the fields, there is a wide range. It is true that all oil-bearing hills have a certain resemblance, due to the formation and to the presence of shale and sandstone, but oftentimes most of the rocks are hidden beneath quaternary deposit of foreign earth, as is the case in Los Angeles, Kern River, all along the Coast and in the Fullerton, Whittier and Puente fields. In the sections named there is in most cases a good growth of vegetation on the hills, with the exception of the Kern River, where poisonous minerals prevent growth. There are other cases where a vast amount of gypsum and sulphur are spread over the hills, giving a lighter color and hiding the formation.

There are cases where the formation is regular, as is the case along the northeastern foothills of the Coast Range, all the way from Sunset to the He Wall, and there are other cases, notably Oil City, where the formation is so irregular that no stratum follows a direct course for a rod and no description can give an edequate conception of the contortions of the rocks.

Fortunately, there is an economy in nature, and with the exceptions of Los Angeles and Summerland, I do not know of an oil district in which the land has any particular value aside from the new industry. In the Orange county district and along the coast it is true that the hills furnished precarious picking for cattle and a possible living for sheep, but only a trifle of the land was tillable. As for the hills along the San Joaquin Valley where the oil has been found, in the Kern River, as well as other fields, more desolate regions are not to be found in California, and in most cases it would be difficult to grow enough feed for a bird on an acre of ground.

OIL INDICATIONS

What are the indications of the presence of oil? There have been many theories, and like others I have been carried away by some of them. But when all has been said, it appears the only real indications of oil which the best judges are inclined to accept while there is such an abundance of territory are oil seepages and oil sand.

Oil seepages are manifest by a deposit of asphaltum, which is the residuum after the oil has evaporated. There is a difference, it seems to me, in the value of asphaltum as an index to oil between a live seepage and an old deposit. The theory used to be generally accepted that where the deposit of asphaltum is great the oil would be found to be very heavy, and where there was no seepage there would be light oil. This was based on the supposition that if any of the oil could escape, most of the gas would have found its way out. But the districts where there are heaviest deposits of asphaltum are Brea Canyon, Ventura county, and McKittrick, but each of those sections produces light oil, while Summerland, Los Angeles and Kern River, where there is little or no asphaltum, produce heavy oil.

Oil is found confined in sand or sandstone. This may be of coarse or fine texture. The only relationship the sand has to the oil is that one furnishes a reservoir for the other, and the oil enters any kind of sand or light gravel that is at hand. Over this sand there is usually a stratum of blue shale, which, being but baked clay or crockery, is capable of preventing a seepage of oil. I do not know of a district in the State where oil has been found but oil sand is to be found exposed. The finest exhibit of it in Los Angeles is at the corner of Alvarado and Eighth streets.

Usually the sand is seen simply as a portion of the soil, and the careless observer might overlook it, taking it for adobe, which it sometimes resembles in color, though of an oily black or chocolate brown. I have never seen oil sand in place as a well-defined stratum of any considerable size except in one case. It is quite frequently seen, particularly in the Whittier district, as a narrow outcropping between other strata, but its full width is not there revealed. The one exception I make is a remarkable stratum of the sand which extends for miles through portions of San Luis Obispo and Santa Barbara counties. I traced it for nearly three miles and heard of the same stratum at a number of points. It is on this stratum that Tom Hughes of Los Angeles is locating a strong company just over the Santa Ynez Mountains from Lompoc. There Mr. Hughes found a place where the stratum had been broken by an earthquake some time in the remote past, and the crack in the earth thus created had been at once filled with oil, which left the crack full of asphaltum. The suddenness with which this was filled is shown by the fact that the two sides of the crack correspond exactly with each other.

The stratum to which I allude is between 200 and 300 feet in thickness and is in place as perfectly as any stratum of rock to be seen in the country.

It would be too much to say that there is no oil except where these manifestations are made by nature. I have seen a number of places where there was a strong odor of oil in the sands, though I could not find the true color, and at least a small amount of oil has been found in such places. It would seem as though where the gases are undoubtedly escaping from the oil there ought to be a good prospect, and it is encouraging to know that several companies are sinking wells in those districts. Their experience will be valuable as determining to what extent the odor goes in pointing to the presence of oil, but meanwhile most operators ask to see the sand of asphaltum before putting in their money.

WAGES OF EMPLOYEES

The growth of the oil industry has brought to the State a great number of drillers from Colorado, Pennsylvania and other States. It might be thought that the increased demand for skilled men would result in a shortage of supply, but such is not the case. There are not many idlers around the oil districts, but there appears to be some more than enough men to meet all requirements. Wages in the oil districts range from $2 to $5 per day, as a rule, with a few exceptional cases where $6 is paid to expert drillers. Thus, directly, the effect of the industry has been to disburse thousands of dollars daily, and the indirect benefit has been scarcely less, for the supplies demanded, in the way of lumber, iron work, etc., have given employment to many other well-paid men in other lines.

CAPITALIZING COMPANIES

The State is passing through an era of capitalization of corporations, and among the companies being organized there are those of all grades of good and evil, requiring the most careful vigilance on the part of investors. There are hundreds of men who are endeavoring to get a foothold in the new industry without the expenditure of capital. But with it all, there are many companies organized on a legitimate basis, from whom great achieveents are expected. California is now paralleling the experience of Pennsylvania during the sixties in this respect, and it is hardly to be expected that even the majority of the investors who take a part in the development of the industry will come out winners. But there have already been seen many who have in a short time made fortunes from oil with small investments, and this is apt to be repeated many times in the years to come, though the successes of the minority will contribute no great comfort to the majority who are destined to lose. The precautions which all the best newspapers are urging on the people along this line are not discouraging to the careful investor, but are given as warning to those who are paying their money over to promoters of companies without themselves taking any pains to ascertain the truth of the claims made.

TRANSPORTATION

The production of oil is one thing and getting it to the market is another. Every city and town in the State is making demands for the new fuel, but before it can be laid down before the factory there must be some means provided for transporting it. It must be said to the credit of both railroads that they are lending their facilities to the growth of the industry, throwing out spurs to new districts, even before the business in sight is sufficient to insure large profits. But many of the producers are looking to securing independence of the railroads by the establishment of pipe lines to the coast. The oil of some of the districts is so heavy that it is questionable whether it would be practicable to undertake to pipe it, but from other districts this can be done successfully.

There are a number of pipe lines now in existence, the largest of which is that of the Union Oil Company, taking in the oils of the Whittier, Brea Canyon and Fullerton fields, which is taken by gravity to San Pedro and thence sent by steamer to San Francisco. The Puente Company has a pipe line for carryig its oil forty-five miles across country to the refinery at Chino, and through the State there are a number of shorter pipe lines, conducting oil from the fields to the railroads.

That the number of pipe lines will be increased is certain, and the inexpensive process of pumping oil to the seaboard can be expected to prevail generally wherever that is possible.

THE FUTURE

With all that has been and can be said regarding the magnitude of the industry, the fact remains that it is yet but in its infancy. The people of California are approaching the subject with a realization of the magnitude of the task before them and with a comprehension of the opportunities which it opens, and yet the greatest need of the day is a better knowledge of the details of the oil business as presented in California. Those who are familiar with the industry in other States are lost here, and the scientists are able to give nothing more valuable than generalities. The field is ripe for the student of practical oil development. It is a rich opportunity which is presented to the young man. It is an opportunity which will give him a scope for the energies of a long life. He may be able eventually to glean and systematize knowledge the lack of which makes it difficult for any person to present a comprehensive outline of the great and growing new industry.

EDGAR F. HOWE.

Los Angeles County

IN THE amount of oil production to the present time Los Angeles county stands easily at the head in the State. Some years more than three-fourths of the entire output of the State has been produced in Los Angeles county.

The county embraces four distinct fields, the Newhall, Los Angeles city, Whittier and Puente. The latter two are classed as different fields, although in conformation of the ground, in the trend of the hills, in the depth of the wells and the gravity of the oil, the two might as well be classed as one district. This similarity does not exist in other districts, and for this reason they are treated under different heads. As the most important oil field in the county, the Los Angeles city field is considered first.

LOS ANGELES FIELD

While the Los Angeles City oil field was not the first to be discovered or operated in Los Angeles county, it has been by far the most important in point of production. The Pico Canyon wells in the Newhall field antedated Los Angeles by nearly twenty years, and the Puente wells were pumping for eight years before the first productive well was opened in this city. But it was not for lack of prospecting that oil was not discovered sooner. Thousands of dollars had been expended and a great many wells sunk before the lucky men finally struck the right spot and opened the first well in this city. As far back as 1863 a well was drilled on Hoover street, between Seventh street and Wilshire boulevard, by the late Mr. Baker, of the Baker Block, and others. The enterprise is said to have cost the promoters no less than $65,000, an expensive expert having been sent for a protracted trip through the East to investigate the oil business, the greater portion of the money going for "incidental expenses." This was undoubtedly the first well drilled in Los Angeles city, if not the first in Southern California. Several army officers were interested in this enterprise.

For thirty years, prospecting for oil in the city continued with varying success. At times small quantities of oil would be found, but owing to lack of market and ignorance of the true value of the fluid, no substantial progress was made. In 1873 D. Ellsworth, who has been a successful oil operator, drilled a well near the corner of Coronado and Fourth streets. He found some oil and considerable water. Other wells were sunk in various portions of the city, but the history of the oil industry in Los Angeles began in the fall of 1892, when Messrs. Doheny and Connon sunk a shaft at the corner of Patton and State streets, where brea outcroppings could be discerned. At a depth of 150 feet some oil was found, and a seven-inch hole was drilled in the bottom of the shaft to a depth of 225 feet. The well was a small producer for two or three years, and laid the foundation for the wonderful oil industry of the city.

A VIEW IN THE LOS ANGELES CITY FIELD. Graham Photographer

From that small beginning the industry grew in four years until a production of 4000 barrels daily was maintained, and today, after eight years have elapsed, the industry has to its credit more than seven million barrels and about 700 wells are producing a monthly average of 100,000 barrels.

An important epoch in the history of the city of Los Angeles was marked when Messrs. Doheny and Connon began with pick and shovel to dig an oil well at the corner of Patton and State streets, near the Second street park. It meant a new industry for the city, which would bring millions of dollars to its citizens. It meant the stimulation and building up of old industries, some of which had begun to languish. It meant cheap fuel, the lack of which had always been a material hindrance to the growth of the city. It meant the building up of a large number of manufacturing enterprises. It meant regular employment for hundreds of men, both directly and indirectly, whose weekly and monthly pay roll would add much to the prosperity of the city.

The first well being sunk in such a primitive manner, was, of course, of necessity not a great success, but it proved the existence of oil in paying quantities, and the drilling of wells with suitable machinery, both by the discoverers of the oil and others, began rapidly. During the first three years after the discovery of oil about three hundred wells were sunk. The growth of the field was, at first, towards the east, as it was considered that the best oil territory lay in that direction. From the proximity of the drilling to the Second street park the oil district took its name, and was for several years known as "The Second-street Park Oil District," and not as the Los Angeles city district, as at present, when the field extends almost entirely across the city. When the line of derricks had reached Victor street on the east, a break in the formation was encountered, and oil men believed that they had reached the end of the stratum. They then turned back to Second street park and started westward with their operations.

In the meantime operations in the territory lying between the Sisters' Hospital and Catholic Cemetery had been begun. This territory, being east of the break at Victor street, had not been considered available for oil purposes. Oil men were one day surprised to learn that a new field had been opened up in the city. This oil belt is quite narrow, in places being not more than 200 feet wide, but, while it lasted, was the scene of the greatest activity of any portion of the oil developments in the city. The oil is of the lightest gravity found in the city, and for this reason, together with the fact that the stratum was so narrow and the dip so steep, the oil was quickly pumped out and the stratum exhausted. During the months of October, November and December, 1897, 100 new wells were opened. It was during this year that the production of petroleum in this city reached its maximum, the amount being estimated at 1,400,000 barrels. The growth of the western city field has been more gradual, but it has gradually advanced to the west line of the city and beyond.

Briefly described, the geological boundaries of the Los Angeles oil fields are as follows: Beginning at the Catholic Cemetery on Buena Vista street, it extends west and slightly south, directly across the city, to a point near the corner of Ocean View avenue and Coronado street, where it turns to the north and crosses Vermont avenue, which is here the western boundary of the city between Third and Fourth streets. West of the city the stratum has been followed for a distance of half a mile, and, although the wells are shallow, they are fair producers. Oil indications are found as far west as Santa Monica, and much prospecting has been done to find the oil sand, but thus far no producing wells are reported farther west than what would be an extension of Western avenue, nor farther south than Fourth street. Neither has oil yet been found east of the Los Angeles River, although many efforts to find it have been made. It is the opinion of many that the Los Angeles oil belt is a continuation of the oil found at Whittier and Puente, but this remains to be proven.

In its course across the city, the oil belt is from a block to two blocks in width, and nature seems to have set definite limitations on a north and south extension. On the north line, where the oil sand is nearer the surface, the wells have proved unproductive, the oil seeming to have dried out. On the south line there seems to be a break in the formation, or perhaps a sharp fold in the stratum. Wells drilled too far south have usually resulted in finding water.

The Los Angeles oil district is usually referred to as divided into three sections, known as the East, Central and West fields. A more correct division would give four sections, as follows: The East field, extending from the Catholic Cemetery to the Sisters' Hospital grounds; the Central or Second-street Park field, extending from Victor street to Belmont avenue; the Nob Hill section, from Belmont to Coronado, and the West, or Baptist College field, embracing everything west of Coronado. Each of these sections have marked characteristics. In the east field the wells are shallow, drilling easy, the oil of light gravity and the oil belt narrow. The wells have not been long lived, and the territory is now considered almost pumped out. A few wells have been deepened with moderate success in increasing the flow, but as no second oil sand is known to exist here, it is not thought that the section will long continue to produce. The wells were placed so closely together that the oil sand was quickly drained of the brown fluid. The custom of placing the derricks so close together has been general throughout the city, and was caused by the fact that every man was eager to pump as much oil from his own property as possible, and when his neighbor drilled two wells, he was compelled to do likewise in self-defense. This has resulted in the drilling of two wells on one small lot in many places, and, as a consequence, has shortened the life of the industry in the city.

The Central or Second-street Park district is the oldest and thus far the most productive in the city. Its wells have continued to produce for a number of years. A second and deeper oil sand is found here, and wells which were put down in 1893 are still producing a limited amount of oil, and give promise of continuing for some time yet.

The Nob Hill tract furnishes the deepest wells and the hardest drilling. From the depth of the wells and the thickness of the oil sands this section is considered the best in the city.

The West or Baptist College field, has, within the past year, produced immense quantities of oil, probably one-third of the total output of the city. Drilling is easy, the wells shallow, ranging from 250 to 500 feet in depth, and the sand is heavy with oil. Only the first sand has thus far been tapped, but as it is more than 100 feet thick it has been a tremendous producer. A second sand is believed to underlie this field, but has not yet been exploited. If it proves as good as the first sand, the field will have a long life, but unless this is found to be true, the rapidity with which the wells are being put down must necessarily exhaust the present sand.

The depth at which oil is found varies considerably in different portions of the field. On Nob Hill some of the wells are 1400 feet deep, and on the Maltman tract, west and south of the Baptist College, the wells average less than 250 feet in depth. The various strata encountered in the wells vary almost as much as the depth. However, in general it may be said that the rock penetrated consists of soft sandstones, sandy clays, and shales, which are interstratified by limestone and calcareous strata and two or more strata of oil-bearing sand. All fossils found in the outcroppings from rocks in the Los Angeles oil field belong to the Pliocene age. In some portions of the field the principal strata encountered before entering the oil sand is a clay shale. The oil sand varies in thickness from 50 feet to 150 feet. From about the point where the oil strike crosses Temple street and extending westward, two oil-bearing strata have been found, each about 100 feet in thickness and separated by a stratum of clay shale. The lower oil stratum is the richer in oil and gas and of a higher degree of gravity. East of Temple street efforts to find the second oil sand have not been successful. The average angle or "dip" of the oil sand is about 40 degrees, and generally to the south, although as in nearly everything else pertaining to Los Angeles oil wells, there is little uniformity. In some places a dip of 16 degrees has been found. Of course, where the dip is greatest the field is most restricted, but in no place does the width of the oil belt extend more than the distance of two city blocks.

While there is no method of determining exactly the amount of oil produced by the Los Angeles oil field, for the reason that in the earlier days of production there was no organization of the oil producers, yet by those whose means of acquiring the information is most accurate, the total amount produced to the present time is estimated at 6,782,000 barrels. There was a little oil produced in 1892, but as the wells were started late in the fall, the amount produced is inconsiderable and is considered as a portion of the output of the next year. The following is the production by years:

	Barrels.
1893	100,000
1894	400,000
1895	900,000
1896	1,200,000
1897	1,400,000
1898	1,182,000
1899	1,200,000
1900 (to date, Sept. 1, 1900)	800,000
Total	7,182,000

It will be seen that the high-water mark was reached in 1897. For a number of months during that year the daily production was in excess of 4,000 barrels. For the past two years the average daily production has been close to 3,500 barrels, the number of new wells, with a large production when first opened, being an offset to the shrinkage of the old wells.

The average price received for the oil during the seven years has been 85 cents per barrel. The price has fluctuated considerably since the beginning of the industry. Owing to the rapid increase of production in 1895, together with the almost entire lack of storage facilities, and lack of co-operation among the producers, the price of oil dropped to a minimum of 25 cents per barrel. This price ruled for a short time only, but the price was generally low for several months. The extra production having been absorbed and the demand increasing, a price of about $1 per barrel ruled throughout 1896. In March, 1897, the demand exceeded the supply, and the price rose to $1.65 per barrel, but the enormous production of that year sent the price down again, for a short time, to a minimum of 50 cents a barrel. Since that time the price has been reasonably stable in the neighborhood of one dollar per barrel. At present, (September 1, 1900), $1.25 is the ruling price. The stability and increase of price is due to the increased facilities for storage and to a better organization of the oil producers, as well as increased demand.

The average cost of wells in the Los Angeles field is estimated at about $2300, but it varies greatly in various portions of the district. In the old Second-street Park field the wells cost about $2500. On Nob Hill the cost runs from $4500 to $5000, and in the western of Baptist College field, wells have been completed at a cost of $800, and the average in that locality is probably less than $1000. The total number of producing wells in the city is now 740. The total number since the beginning of the industry is 1365.

PUENTE

Rising at the west bank of the San Gabriel river in the southwestern part of Los Angeles county and stretching thence, east by south, to the Santa Ana river, a distance of twenty-five miles, lie the Puente Hills. For a portion of the distance, the hills make the boundary line between Orange and Los Angeles counties, and it was here that some of the first successful explorations for oil were made in this part of the state. The exact spot lies seven miles north of the town of Fullerton on the Santa Fe railroad and four miles south of Puente station on the Southern Pacific.

The geological formation of these hills is largely uniform, but few differences except such as are caused by variations in altitude, being noticeable. An igneous surface rock overlaying a bed of shale is the usual formation. Very little rock other than sandstone is found below the surface, although in some of the wells pockets of large boulders have been met with. Thus it happens that although the different localities in the hills are known by various names it is conceded that the oil belt is really the same, whether found at Puente, where the oil was originally discovered, at Whittier on the east, or Brea canyon or Soquel canyon on the west.

The history of the original Puente field is the history of one organization, the Puente Oil Company. Operations were begun by William Lacy about fifteen years ago. The Puente comppany succeeded to his property and now owns about one thousand acres in the Puente ranch, and about three thousand acres of adjoining land, in line with the known oil belt. The company has drilled more than sixty wells, and is now pumping about fifty. A few of the sixty wells have been dry holes, and a few on the outer edge of the belt have ceased to yield remuneratively but some of the wells nearly fifteen years old are still pumping daily.

The developed oil field of the Puente Oil Company lies a little south of the crest of the hills from which it takes its name. The dip of the oil formation is from northwest to southeast and the prevailing angle is about forty-five degrees. The average depth of the wells is 1200 feet, and the average cost is $5000.

The Puente company has produced in its history a million and a half barrels of oil. The production for 1899 was 120,112 barrels, and the average for the past five years has been about this figure. Some of the wells have had a phenomenal output. In 1899 one well produced 20,800 barrels and a few years since one well produced more than 50,000 barrels during the first year of its history, an average of 1000 barrels a week. Most of the oil is very light, ranging from 30 to 35 gravity.

During its early operations, the Puente Oil Company marketed its product in Los Angeles city, first piping from its field to the Southern Pacific tracks at Puente and sending into this city by cars. When the great flood of oil was struck in Los Angeles in 1894, it became necessary for it to find another market. It accordingly made a six-years' contract with the Chino Valley Beet Sugar Company to furnish it with fuel for its sugar refinery. A sixteen-mile, three-inch pipe line was laid from the Puente hills to the beet factory, and beginning with the year 1895, the Puente Oil Company has furnished all of the oil used at Chino, which, during some seasons, ran close to 100,000 barrels.

In 1895 the company built a refinery at Chino, and from the time it began operations it ran all of its oil through its refinery, and furnished the Chino sugar factory the residuum. The company has its refinery adjacent to the factory, and storage capacity for about 100,000 barrels, in which it has held the residuum, from the refinery, and delivered during the sugar campaign to the factory.

The refined product is all contracted for by the Standard Oil Company, and in 1899 was as folows:

	Gallons.
Gasoline	130,000
Illuminating oil	500,000
Distillate	1,000,000
Painter's benzine	25,000

The land of the company has been exploited so that territory is now known to exist which will furnish remunerative drilling for at least five years. Developments at the south of the Puente ranch, in the Brea canyon region, have developed at least two additional miles of territory along the southern edge of its holdings.

WHITTIER

The Whittier oil field is the latest to be developed in Los Angeles conuty, but unless all indications are deceptive the district will soon rank among the best, not only of LosAngeles county but of the state. Theis district lies about twenty miles southeast of the city of Los Angeles and is directly adjacent to the beautiful town of Whittier on the north and east. The conformation of the hills and the geological formation of the country seem to make it certain that this district is merely the western extension of the Puente district, which lies five miles directly east.

The fact that the development of the Whittier field is of comparatively recent date has not been for lack of previous prospecting. Twelve years ago when Whittier was in its infancy, the first attempt at oil development was made. Following the successful development of the Puente Oil Company, a few miles to the eastward, a similar attempt was made at Whittier. In the fall of 1888 the Pieckering Land and Water Company, the original company of Whittier, began development in Turnbull canyon in the Puente hills northeast of the town. Three holes were put down with every indication of success, when a drunken contractor "shot" the wells with several pounds of nitro-glycerine and completely destroyed about $14,000 of work. The company became discouraged and ceased operations. Recent developments indicate that the oil belt extends the full length of the range on the line where the original company began operations, and it is evident that if they had not have become discouraged, the Whittier oil field would have been in operation for several years. The hills at Whittier are somewhat rugged, and in many places the upheaval has been so severe that much difficulty has been experienced in sinking wells. These difficulties have been more or less overcome by experience, so that less time is now consumed in sinking a well than formerly. Water frequently develops to an extent that much trouble is experienced in shutting it off, although no wells have had to be abandoned on that account. Not enough water has been developed to be of much use in operations. It is rather hard to approximate the expense of sinking and casing wells. Some have been put down for as little as $3,000. It would be safe to say that $5,000 or $6,000 would be a fair average. The development known as the Chandler wells were a part of the early effort to find oil in the Whittier district. They were sunk before the territory was sufficiently understood to do successful work, and were too small both in depth and diameter, to afford a fair test of the territory. They produced a few barrels of oil daily of low gavity for a while, but were afterward abandoned.

To the Central Oil Company is really due the credit for demostrating the true worth of the Whittier territory. This work was first begun late in the fall of 1896. The company was organized by the election of W. W. Neuer, president; Senator Robert N. Bulla, secretary; J. M. Elliott, treasurer; these gentlemen with Charles H.Toll, W. R. Cook, I. B. Newton, R. P. Wade and H. W. Hines are the principal owners of the company. Considerable stock has been sold to the public, but as a large control is held by these well-known business and professional men of Los Angeles, the operations of the concern is in safe hands. The company owns 2700 acres of land in fee simple. Of this 1100 acres are believed by experts to be good oil territory. There are three well-defined oil strikes on the land of an aggregate length of six miles. On these may be put about 800 wells. The land is 900 feet above tide water, 700 feet above railroad tracks, three miles from the tracks, eighteen miles from San Pedro Harbor, affording the cheapest means of transportation. A steel pipe line runs from the wells to storage tanks at Los Nietos station. Every facility is provided for the economical handling of the output of the wells, so that 1500 barrels a day could

IN THE WHITTIER FIELD SHOWING WELLS OF FIDELITY, TURNER, HOME AND WHITTIER CRUDE OIL COMPANIES.

be shipped at a cost not exceeding 1 cent per barrel. The company has twenty-five producing wells. It has four strings of tools at work, night and day, sinking new wells. These wells are among the heaviest producers in Southern California. The actual output now is 12,000 barrels per month, or an average of 500 per month for each well. A pumping station at the East Whittier company's reservoir forces water to the top of the hill to a large tank, from which it is distributed throughout the entire camp. The camp is made up of boarding houses and private dwellings of employees, blacksmith shop, etc. The Central company has two large pumping jacks in operation. Oil from the wells is forced to a large tank, built on one of the highest hills, from whence it is carried by gravity through a 4-inch pipe line to the junction of the Southern Pacific and Santa Fe at Los Nietos, three and one-half miles from the field. It is received here in two large tanks, and the tank cars are loaded by means of pumps. In 1899 more than 500 car loads were shipped from this point.

The Home Oil Company is the second oil producer of the district, its production being about 5000 barrels per month. As indicated by the name, the company is a local corporation and has been made a success by the efforts of a number of the residents of Whittier. The officers are W. V. Coffin, president; F. H. Buckmaster, vice-president; Alva Starbuck, secretary and manager; G. E. Little, treasurer. This company commenced operations, in a small way, in the summer of 1897, and after a number of discouragements, has succeeded in finding oil in paying quantities. Wells Nos. 3, 4, 5, 6 are now producing about fifty barrels each a day of 19 gravity oil. Drilling has commenced on well No. 7 and No. 8 will begin at once. The company is paying a monthly dividend of 2½ per cent. The lease comprises eighty acres adjoining the town on the east.

The Turner Oil Company, which is composed of M. W. and H. C. Turner, G. W. Brookins and J. T. Kirkwood, has twenty acres lying east of the Home company. Operations were begun in July of last year, and five wells are now producing, with two strings of tools constantly at work. The Turner company hauls its product to the storage tank at the Evergreen depot. The wells of this company are easily and quickly put down, and are not troubled with water.

The Fidelity Oil Company, whose land lies east of the Turner company, is owned by Thomas O'Donnell and Ellis T. Yarnell of Los Angeles, R. T. Harris of Santa Ana, and J. C. McComb and S. E. McKee of Whittier. The company has three producing wells and keeps one string of tools constantly at work. The Whittier Crude Oil Company, formerly the Sale & Off Company, has four producing wells on lease, north of the Home Oil Company. The Warner Oil Company is located on forty acres of the Central main field, on the Savage tract. The company is composed of Charles Warner, of Franklin, Pa.; Isaac Collins, R. J. McClure and W. L. Stafford of Whittier. Well No. 1 when completed at a depth of 1100 feet produced fifty barrels of oil per day. Wells Nos. 2 and 3 were equally good. The product is handled through the Central company's pipe line. The Murphy Oil Company has been exploring new territory south of the Central company's ground. The Clarendon Heights Company is developing good territory in Savage and Worsham canyons.

The North Whittier Oil Company, recently organized by J. W. Hellman, M. W. Hellman, W. W. Neuer, R. N. Bulla, J. T. Sartori and T. E. Newlin of Los Angeles, and H. R. Lacy of Pasadena, is operating on 320 acres of leased land lying directly north of the city. Active development has begun on what promises to be one of the best locations on this end of the range. The Home, Crude, Whittier, Fidelity and Turner companies maintain a pumping plant at the city water works reservoir, and force water to the field. The Home company has its own pipe line, direct to the Southern Pacific road, where oil is loaded to the tank cars from the largest corrugated iron tank in the State.

The Union Oil Company contemplates running branch pipe lines into the Whittier fields, connecting with the Brea canyon lines, running to San Pedro, thus giving, by reason of this and other lines, direct connections with both railroads and the tank steamers. The wagon trade is very extensive, oil being hauled from Whittier to Compton, Downey, Norwalk, Santa Ana, La Mirada, El Monte, Puente and Newmark. By rail the product is shipped all over the southern part of the state. The prevailing price at the wells is $1 to $1.05 per barrel.

NEWHALL

The term Newhall District is rather generic and is used to describe that portion of the northwestern section in Los Angeles county in which are located Pico, Placerita, Elsmere, Wiley and other canyons where oil explorations are going on. The field is one of the oldest in the state. It is situated about thirty miles north of the city of Los Angeles in the San Fernando mountains.

What is known to be about the first producing well in California was put down in 1875 by a company consisting of C. A. Mentry, now superintendent of the Pacific Coast Oil Company's field at Newhall; D. C. Scott and Christopher Leaming. Mr. Mentry, who was an old Pennsylvania driller, put down the first well with a spring pole and got a good flow of oil at thirty-five feet. This well is located in Pico canyon, about seven miles from Newhall in a westerly direction. The same company put down two other wells, but in 1876 sold out their interests to the California Star Oil Company of San Francisco. In June, 1876, this company put up the first standard rig that was set up in the Pico canyon, and began work on the now famous No. 4 well. This is the most famous well in the world, having produced more than one and one half million barrels of oil since it was struck twenty-three years ago and does not show any sign of giving out. From that time on there has been a gradual but steady increase in the development of the Pico territory.

In 1879 the Pacific Coast Oil Company began operating in the Pico field with decided success. Their production is estimated at 130,000 to 150,000 barrels a year. In the 80's the Pacific Coast Oil Company began developing in the Wiley canyon and in the Elsmere district, but with poor success. In fact, these places, after two or three wells were put down in each, were given up and nothing done until recently. Within the last two years the company has resumed work in this section and seems to have struck the oil sand in every hole sunk and has added several more good wells to its

100 BARREL GUSHER WHITE OIL (50 DEG. GRAVITY). PROPERTY OF THE NEW CENTURY OIL CO. AT NEWHALL.

list. In the Elsmere canyon about twelve wells have been put down and oil struck in each one. This company has a pipe line from its wells in the Pico canyon to its wharf in Ventura. This line is fourty-four miles long and consists of twenty miles of 2-inch pipe and twenty-four miles of 4-inch pipe. Their local lines consist of about thirty miles of 2-inch pipe, running from the Elsmere and Wiley districts to the different places of loading, and from Pico to the pumping station from which the company derives its water supply.

The Newhall district or at least that portion of it lying in Placerita canyon has the distinction of producing a quality of oil different from any that is found in any other place in the world, oil sufficiently refined in its natural state to burn well in an ordinary lamp, oil almost as clear when taken from the ground as ordinary kerosene. About six years ago George W. Freeman and Frank Nelson, two prospectors who were sinking for gold in Placerita canyon, were everywhere met by quantities of natural gas, the flow being frequently so strong as to drive them out of their shafts. Finally they decided to cease sinking for gold and drill for oil. With a spring pole and a small drill they sunk the first well and were rewarded after many hardships and months of patient toil with a fine flow of oil, different from anything ever found in the state, if not in the entire world. The oil discovered was nearly 50 degrees gravity and about the color of ordinary kerosene. It is a marvel to all beholders, as it can be used either for engine distillate of for illuminant without refining. Other wells drilled with more effective machinery to a greater depth have only verified the wonders of the first strike. For several months the output of the wells has continued undiminished. The oil is worth $4 to $5 a barrel at the well. The Pioneer White Oil Company are developing a large part of this tract, with every indication of success, and have a large well sunk 500 feet, which shows up great quantities of gas, and a heavy flow of white oil is looked for any day. As this book goes to press the New Century Oil Company has just struck a similar well of this wonderful white oil on adjacent property, which started gushing at the rate of 100 barrels daily. A number of companies are working in the same neighborhood and the district for at least twelve miles in length is busy with active oil development extending from the head of Placerita canyon on the east to the Ventura county line on the west. At the present time, however, there is but one really extensive producer of oil, the Pacific Coast Oil Company.

The New Century Oil Company, encouraged by their recent strike, are now actively engaged in sinking other wells in the immediate vicinity, from which they have every reason to expect equally favorable results.

The officers of the New Century Oil Company are practical business men of Los Angeles. They are C. W. Smith, president; H. O. Haines, Treasurer; F. C. Melton, Secretary. These, with E. S. Bonbright and J. E. Curry, comprise the board of directors.

The oil taken from the Pico wells is of 42 degrees gravity, while that of the White Oil district is said to exceed 50 degrees gravity. That of the Elsmere wells is from 28 to 32 degrees gravity.

As all the oil that is produced by the Pacific Coast Oil Company's wells is shipped in tank steamers to their refinery at Alameda Point and as none is sold at the wells, it is hard to say what price it would bring on the market. But little information concerning this company is obtainable.

Among the promising new fields of oil territory, the Palomas mining district, lying adjacent to the Pico Canyon territory in the Newhall district, is rapidly coming to the front. It is in this territory that the Pacific Coast Oil Company has been producing oil for more than twenty years, and where, at more recent date, the famous White Oil wells have been found. At no place in the State are the wells as long-lived as in the Pico Canyon neighborhood, and experts who have examined the entire district declare that the same kind of wells will also be found in the Palomas territory.

One of the companies organized to drill for oil in the Palomas district is the Prudential Mining and Oil Development Co., which is capitalized for $750,000, with a par value of $1 each. The officers of the company are as follows: Frederick W. Blanchard, President; Lionel V. Redpath, Vice-President; Harvey H. Cox, Secretary, and Charles W. Fleming, Treasurer, all of whom are prominent business men of Los Angeles. The company has a thirty-year lease on 1040 acres of land and is preparing to prosecute vigorous development.

The following letter from the mining expert who examined the property is a brief description of the territory:

James M. Pearson, M. E., says of this district as follows:

Prudential Mining and Oil Development Company:

Gentlemen: On the 16th of May I carefully examined the south half of section 32 north, range 16 west, San Bernardino meridian, said property being located in the Palomas Mining District, Los Angeles county, 8½ miles north of Castiac Station, on the Southern Pacific Railway.

Upon examination I found a perfect oil-bearing formation, which extends for many miles. The formation consists of calcareous sandstone, black, brown and blue shale, gypsum, blue clay and sand strata. The gypsum is interspersed in the brown shale. The black shales are a species of hydrocarbons which are known to yield oil. The surface rocks are coal measures or lower carboniferous sandstone. The stratification is so perfect and well defined that the anticlinal is readily traced, the trend of which is south of west and north of east, and can be traced for many miles. The stratographical and topographical conditions of your property are positive indications of oil.

In the mountains north of your property I found a well-defined strata of soft, black, bituminous shale. Limestone and black marcellus shale strata next below the limestone. There is no difficulty in tracing the shale strata. These shales manifest a predisposition to the production of oil. In this district such shales are abundant, judging from the formation and all indications, it is my opinion that large producing wells can be developed on your property, and that the oil, when struck, will not be less than 36 specific gravity.

I find that section 27 in the same township and range is identically the same as section 32 in formation.

Yours respectfully, JAMES M. PEARSON, M. E.

The Mullen & Bluett flowing well on section 18, township 6 north, range 15 west, S. B. M., is one further proof that the Palomas district is among the very choicest and most productive fields in the entire State. An especially favorable feature in this well is the high specific gravity, which, as all know, greatly increases the value of the oil. The proof of this is found in the fact that this particular oil of 36 gravity sells readily at prices varying from $3 to $3.50 per barrel.

The formations encountered in putting down this well evidence the fact that a great and steady flow may be looked for—one which may be depended upon to last for many years, with the same productiveness which has now continued for more than three years.

On section 19, township 6 north, range 15 west, McCracken & Hulburt are making extensive preparations to sink their first well. Being in the center of so productive a district, in which they own and control large acreage, there seems every reasonable possibility of their meeting with a successful result.

Another company located in this promising section is the Reliance, which has property as follows: Eighty acres in the famous White Oil district at Newhall, 880 acres in the Palomas District, on which the company is now operating. The company also has 80 acres leased in the Buckhorn district, where good production is obtained at depths varying from 150 to 500 and 600 to 1000-barrel wells are obtained at from 850 to 1000 feet. All these lands have been thoroughly experted by experienced oil men. The officers of the company are Frank H. Landall, President; E. J. Brown, Superintendent; R. Y. Campton, Secretary.

OFFICERS AND MEMBERS OF THE GOVERNING BOARD LOS ANGELES OIL EXCHANGE.

The Washington Oil Company is another promising organization in this territory, with officers as follows: N. A. Wolcott, President; George R. E. Milligan, Vice-President; Malcolm McMartin, Superintendent; M. F. Ginder, Secretary, and George S. Clarke, Director. The company controls 2080 acres two miles from the Mullen & Bluett well, and believed to be on the same strata formation. The property lies five miles north of the Castiac Station on the Southern Pacific Railroad. The company is capitalized for $5,000,000, with shares of a par value of $1 each.

LOS ANGELES OIL EXCHANGE

The Los Angeles Oil Exchange is the only organization in the State, dealing in oil securities, which has had uninterrupted success from the beginning, or which may be classed as really prosperous at present. Other institutions, both in this city and in San Francisco, are doing business but without the same degree of success. The exchange was organized during the month of December, 1899, in order to promote the oil industry, and the investment of capital in oil properties, make a market value for oil securities, and become the medium of investments in oil securities and industries. The success which has attended the exchange and the growing favor in which it is received by the public are evidences of the wisdom of its organizers.

The first call on the exchange was made February 1, 1900, and regular calls have been held every day since. The volume of business has grown steadily month by month as will be shown by the following figures: February business, $15,514.18; March business, $32,430.75; April business, $74,066.95; May business, $160,196.45; June business, $141,464.83; July business, $95,-179.11; August business, $119,461.95. Total for seven months, $638,314.22.

In the beginning the membership of the exchange was limited to fifty but as interest and enthusiasm grew, this number has been increased from time to time until there are now 125 members with a limit of possible membership of 130. The greatest accession of membership was when fifty-one members of the California Oil Exchange relinquished their seats in that body in exchange for seats on the Los Angeles Oil Exchange. It is an interesting fact and well worthy of note that a large number of the members are actual oil producers, and while this continues to be the case the conservative policy which has made the exchange so popular, will be maintained.

At first only stocks of companies which possessed actual producing wells and were known to be safely and conservatively managed, were listed for calling on the board. Later, however, in response to an almost universal popular demand, this was modified by allowing stocks of non-producing companies to be dealt in, but this class of securities is not guaranteed by the exchange. Sales of this kind of stock have not affected the market of the listed stock, the latter securities remaining the favorite of the brokers and the public. In fact, it is now generally considered that by permitting the sales of unlisted securities the public is afforded a protection by the publicity which is drawn to them.

The exchange is located at 115 South Broadway and has large and commodious quarters, which have twice been enlarged to make room for the rapidly-increasing membership and the large number of interested spectators who attend all sessions.

The officers and governing board are as follows: President, Wallace L. Hardison; vice-president, Carl Alexander Johnson; secretary, R. W. Poindexter; treasurer, Louis Blankenhorn, and these with Leonard Merrill, C. A. Sumner and W. H. Axtater, constitute the governing committee.

The rates charged for buying and selling stocks are as follows: Shares selling under 10 cents, 1-4 cent per share; shares selling at 10 cents and under 50 cents, 1-2 cent a share; shares selling above 50 cents, 1 per cent. on par value of stock. A minimum price of $1 is charged on each transaction.

CALIFORNIA OIL AND STOCK EXCHANGE

The California Oil and Stock Exchange is the junior organization in Los Angeles, formed for the purpose of trading in oil securities. It began business April 16, 1900, with more than one hundred members. The exchange is located at 105 South Broadway, where its rooms are admirably adapted to the business, and are beautifully and tastefully arranged and decorated. The business of the exchange has been large and its management is in the hands of some of the leading business and professional men of the city. The officers of the exchange are as follows: John T. Jones, President; D. H. Imler, Vice-President; W. B. Scarborough, Secretary; E. W. Nettleton, Treasurer; George J. Common, Caller.

The California Oil and Stock Exchange was the first to give the public the opportunity of dealing in the stocks of companies which are not yet producing oil. This move was very popular, and the sessions were not only attended by large crowds of interested spectators, but were marked by an immense volume of business. It is expected that the exchange will take an important part, in the future, in the development of the oil industry of California.

Fresno County

COALINGA AND OIL CITY

ALTHOUGH in point of production the Fresno county oil fields are rated among the most recent in the State, yet in the way of prospecting it is many years old. One of the first oil companies in the State was formed to operate in that county. It was known as the Elkhorn Petroleum Company. It is is indeed doubtful if this company does not antedate the Santa Cruz organization, which has the credit of being the first oil corporation in the United States. The Elkhorn was a twenty-year corporation, and if it ever accomplished anything, there is no evidence left of the fact. Prospecting for oil along the east slope of the mountains, which lie along the western boundary of the county, continued at intervals for years, particularly in 1889. The following year a few shallow wells were sunk, but did not find oil in paying quantities. It was not until 1893 that anything of a stir was aroused. Rowland and Lacy, who had opened the wonderful Puente field in Los Angeles county, did some prospecting near Coalinga that year, and announced the belief that the hills contained a rich oil stratum. Their belief was based upon personal investigations, and as they were known to be men of experience, a miniature oil boom was the result. They proceeded to put down a well, and after working several months struck oil in small quantities. The oil was of fairly good quality, but was so limited in quantity that the original prospectors were obliged to abandon their project with the closing of their experimental well, and the little boom died with their retirement. This well, however, was the beginning of the oil development in Fresno county, and was the first put down in what is now the prosperous oil field, of which Oil City, nine miles north of Coalinga, is the recognized center. Nothing farther was attempted in the way of oil development until the spring of 1895, when a couple of wells were put down in what is now the famous "section 20," by the Producers' and Consumers' Oil Company. Both proved good wells. From that time on there has been a steady increase in the development of oil property in that locality, and today the district is one of the best in the State.

There are now so many oil claims in this district that it is a matter of difficulty to keep track of them, and while many of these have never been prospected further than a mere superficial examination, there are many others upon which wells have been sunk and which are producing probably 40,000 barrels of oil per month. The territory in which oil has been found lies almost entirely in three sections of land, the numbers being 17, 20 and 28, township 19 south, range 15 east. In section 17, which is the farthest north that oil has been discovered in this field, the wells are comparatively shallow, ranging from 500 to 600 feet and producing ten to fifteen barrels of oil daily. They were the first wells opened in the district and have been fair producers.

The great wells of the Coalinga field, the promotion of which has given it the reputation of being a district of gushers, are on section 20. The north half of this section is the property of the Coalinga, Home and Blue Goose oil companies. The latter owns the east half of the northeast quarter and has not yet found oil, in paying quantities. The celebrated Blue Goose well, which is today the most famous in the State, is the property of the Home Company. The oil stratum in this section, although marvelously rich, is quite narrow and seems to lie along the dividing line between the northeast and northwest quarters of section 20.

It is now generally conceded and practical experience has demonstrated that the oil in this field trends from the northwest toward the southeast. There are doubtless many strata of oil, some of which come very near the surface in places, one overlying the other, so that as the development proceeds towards the southeast, new strata are struck from time to time, and oil of various gravities is found. On the Coalinga Company's property and on the property of the Home Oil Company there are ten producing wells. These are all flowing wells, which have been piped to tanks near by. From these tanks the oil is taken to the tank cars by pipe line. The wells do not run or flow continuously. The gas is the lifting power, and it is intermittent. The wells will spout and flow steadily for several minutes, until the force of the accumulated gas has become exhausted, and then they will stop. After a quiet period of from ten to twenty minutes, varying usually according to the age of the well, the gas generates in sufficient quantities to force another flow, and the oil comes up again. Eventually these flowing wells will cease to flow, and will then be pumped, the same as the other wells. The oil found is about 35 deg. gravity, which is considered high in California, but so far as known no attempt at refining for illuminating purposes has been made.

In the realm of possibilities for great future development, no district in California offers greater inducements than does the eastern slope of the Coast Range of mountains, west of the Coalinga oil fields. Here are extensive outcroppings of oil sand, on either side of well defined anticlinals; while numerous seepages and oil springs are found at frequent intervals.

Especially is this true of the Warthan Canyon region. This canyon, as it crosses township 21, 13, has been formed by the eroding away of the crest of an anticinal, and all along the sides of the canyon can be seen stratum after stratum of sand that is strongly impregnated with oil. Several oil springs are located near the northwestern end of the township and an extensive seepage is found where the canyon crosses township 21, 14.

In section 24, township 21, 13, the anticlinal leaves the canyon and for a short distance runs unbroken. It is along this unbroken portion that the Coalinga Crude Oil Company owns land that is bound, in time, to make this company one of the strongest oil companies in California.

The company is formed by a number of successful and substantial business men, and their prospects in this and other districts are most flattering.

Officers and Directors—President, W. A. Cooper, General Freight Agent Los Angeles Terminal Railway; Vice-President, W. J. Johnson, of the Bank of Commerce, Albuquerque, N. M.; Secretary, B. A. Bertrand, Los Angeles; Treasurer, J. A. Medlar, of the Gazette Publishing Company, Los Angeles; Attorney, H. C. Brown, Los Angeles; C. C. Hawcroft, Los Angeles; F. H. Redpath, Los Angeles; W. N. Best, Los Angeles, W. J. Beaver, San Bernardino; H. C. Ackerly, Herald Publishing Company, Los Angeles.

VIEW OF A PORTION OF THE OIL CITY WELLS COALINGA DISTRICT

Among the other companies which have large holdings in this immediate vicinity are the New York, Selma, Crescent, Selma Mutual, Oil City Petroleum and Hanford. Many other companies are located within a few miles, but so far as known none have yet found oil. Some of the companies named have struck oil in limited quantities, but there are no good properties to date, except the Home and Coalinga.

The camp is well supplied in the matter of storage and shipping facilities. A pipe line of three-inch pipe, reaching from Oil City to Ora, on the Southern Pacific Railroad, a distance of nine miles, is in operation, and through this line almost all the oil is sent to the tank cars. There is a charge of ten cents per barrel for this service, and when freight is deducted to the San Francisco market there is a net price to the producer at the wells of from 85 cents to $1.15, according to the quality and gravity of the oil. There is not a great deal of oil used in the fields—probably not more than from sixty to seventy-five barrels per day. For this the producers get an average of $1.30 per barrel. The reason a better price is had there than for oil shipped is accounted for by the difficulty of handling it in small quantities at the fields. The storage capacity for oil in the Coalinga and Oil City districts, in large tanks, is about 52,000 barrels capacity, but shipments are almost continuous, and comparatively little oil is stored either at the wells or at the railroad. There is but one oil-pumping outfit in the district, and this belongs to Chanslor & Canfield. This plant is pumping seven wells. It is an eccentric pump, operated by a twenty-horse-power engine. The scarcity of pumping plants is accounted for by the fact that so many of the wells are gushers and do not need the aid of a pump to produce oil.

KREYENHAGEN

The second oil district of Fresno county is the Kreyenhagen country. It lies in the extreme southwestern portion of the county and has not yet produced sufficient oil to be ranked among the producing territories. The district lies about fifteen miles southeast of Coalinga and has the same general trend, not only of the Oil City district on the north, but of the McKittrick and Sunset fields many miles farther south. In fact, many oil men have gone on record in expressing the belief that the eastern slope of the Coast Range contains a continuous oil belt, extending from the Tehachapi through the entire length of the San Joaquin Valley.

The Kreyenhagen district is recorded to have produced the lightest oil yet found in the State in any considerable quantity, but it remains to be proven yet whether or not the oil is to be produced in quantities sufficient for commercial purposes. The first well put down showed oil of 43½ deg. gravity, and an analysis bears out the statement that it comes from a paraffine base, which is in contradistinction from all other oil found in the State (unless it is the white oil of the Newhall district), which has an asphaltum base.

The district takes its name from the fact that the land belongs to four brothers by the name of Kreyenhagen. The owners were at first very reluctant either to sell or lease any land for oil purposes. The first well drilled was a contract well, put down by the Director's Company, and was in the nature of prospecting. E. R. Snyder and J. M. Hendrickson were the pioneer prospectors of the territory, and the Director's Company was organized by them for the purpose of testing the ground.

In all there are a dozen companies operating in this section, but so far as known the Kreyenhagen and Black Mountain companies are the only ones to have found any considerable quantity of oil, and even these companies have none to ship, the output being used on the ground for development purposes. The Kreyenhagen Land and Oil Company controls 480 acres, and the Black Mountain Petroleum Company, 320 acres of the original Kreyenhagen tract, and it is upon this portion of the territory that the best quality of oil has been found up to date. The stock of these companies is largely held in Los Angeles and active work is being prosecuted on both properties.

Among other companies operating in the Kreyenhagen district are the King's County Oil Company, the California Consolidated Petroleum Company, the Stanley, the Baby King, Verona and St. Lawrence.

WELL NO. 2, FULLERTON OIL COMPANY, FULLERTON

Kern County

IT is written that the first shall be last and the last shall be first. When the true and complete story of the oil development of the state is written, it will be recorded that in the same county which had for years been producing oil for refining into asphaltum, there sprang up last year the most wonderful oil boom of the decade. Kern county is large in all respects. It is large in area, which exceeds in size the state of Connecticut. It is great in resources, which include everything in the way of mineral and agricultural wealth. But most of all, Kern county is great in its large-hearted, open-handed, liberal and progressive inhabitants.

To form a proper conception of the size and extent of the Kern county oil fields, one must realize that the county, or at least the greater portion of it, was once the head of a great inland sea, whose eastern shores were on the slopes of the Sierras, whose western waves lapped the crags of the coast range and whose northernmost end extended to the Golden Gate. Extending around the valley in which Bakersfield, the metropolis of Kern county, is situated, at an elevation of about 700 to 1000 feet, the shore line of this inland sea is marked by vast deposits of fossil remains, such as shark's teeth, vertebra and great masses of shells. It is in this shore line, a strip about three miles wide and extending from the east around on the south of the valley on the Sierra Nevada, and coast ranges to the extreme northwestern corner of the county, that the oil discoveries have been made. The extreme length of the semi-circular strip is about sixty miles and it has been exploited in at least four distinct sections in a manner which would indicate that the field is more or less continuous for the whole distance. Geographically speaking, the indications begin in township 27, 28 and 27, 29 on the east, with their greatest development centering in townships 28, 28 and 29, 28 immediately north of the Kern river, and about four miles northeast of Bakersfield. This is the Kern River district. The granite outcroppings of the Sierra Nevadas come out into the valley south of Kern river, and seem to break in the field for some distance until the San Emidio district is reached in township 11, north, ranges 21, 22, 23, 24, west S. B. M. In ranges 21 and 22 of township 11, the outcroppings and surface indications are extremely good and warrant the very large amount of prospecting which is just beginning in these townships.

ON THE KERN RIVER

The Kern River oil district is located about six miles northeast of the town of Bakersfield. The district is the south end of the San Joaquin Valley, a valley 300 miles long and 80 miles in width on an average. About 30 miles south of this district there come together the Sierra Nevada moun-

IN KERN RIVER FIELD SHOWING CAMP AND WELLS OF THE REED CRUDE OIL COMPANY tains and Coast Range. On the north and east extend the Sierra Nevada range with its walls of granite extending to a height of several thousand feet. On the east and west is the Coast Range with its shale, sandstone and lime formation at a somewhat lesser elevation; in other words, there is a dyke impenetrable to oil and extending in a semi-circle around the valley in an easterly, southerly and westerly direction. The Kern River oil district is a basin filled to an unknown depth with loose material such as sand, clay and shale, the sand being saturated with oil and immured above and below with strata of clay.

The whole aspect of the country is such as to impress every visitor to this district that whatever was done by nature must have been done on a grand scale. Kern River district is at an elevation of 400 feet above the sea level; it is at the south end of the largest valley in the State. Scientists have said that the whole San Joaquin Valley was an arm of the Pacific Ocean; an inland sea of salt water, the outlet being the Golden Gate.

The deposits in this immediate vicinity of fossil lime stones are known to exist to a thickness of in some cases 200 feet. There is no other place in California where there is evidence of such a profusion of prehistoric animal and marine life. There is no oil district where the conditions are similar and where one would expect to find such immense deposits of oil as here.

The Discovery of Oil

Oil was discovered on the banks of Kern river about six miles from Bakersfield in May, 1899. The seepage of oil extends along the river bank for a distance of one and one-half miles. There was a well sunk with pick and shovel to a depth of about 60 feet, the diameter being about six feet. In sinking this distance Mr. Elwood, the discoverer, passed through what is called oil sand and when the depth of 60 feet was reached, quite a flow of oil came into the well, so much so that the discovery attracted wide-spread attention. In a few weeks oil men from every part of California came to Bakersfield to inspect the new discovery.

The first derrick was erected in July of last year by E. L. Doheny; the first well was completed sometime in September last. What is known as the "Discovery Well" was drilled to a depth of about 350 feet; this well produced by pumping about 30 barrels of oil a day.

The Present Area

Soon after the discovery was made, locators were scattered over the hills to a distance of 20 or 30 miles in every direction. The concensus of opinion of oil men was, even in the earlier stages of development work, that the strata of oil sand extended in a northwesterly and southeasterly course. Along and on either side of the center of the supposed stratum of oil sand derricks were erected and drillers commenced operations.

Within the past twelve months the time during which development work had been carried on, the territory has been proved in a northwesterly direction about five miles and in a northeasterly and southwesterly direction about four miles, making in all a proven oil territory of about fifteen square miles. The stratum of oil sand to the east along Kern River, was

about twenty feet thick. The thickness of the oil sand continued to increase until the western limits of the territory now presents an average thickness of not less than 300 to 500 feet, and every new well developed in the northwesterly course shows an increased depth of the stratum of oil sand.

Horizontal Stratum

Prof. Joseph LeConte of the University of California, Prof. Whitney of Yale College, and other scientists have said that there never would be found a horizontal stratum of oil sand in the State of California such as was found in Pennsylvania. It was contended by these scientists that the stratum of oil sand would be on an incline similar to that of the more solid formation of the mountain ranges such as contain gold, silver, cinnabar and other minerals. It was also contended that it would be impossible to find in this mountainous district the stratum of oil sand to any great width and for the reason that there being of necessity a dip of the sand, the depth of which would not justify results to be obtained.

The Kern River oil field, however, presents a condition of stratum that plainly contradicts the theory of the scientists.

The stratum of oil sand is almost horizontal, there being, however, a slight dip of the stratum to the west and south; a dip amounting to about 120 feet to the mile.

The discovery well, as already said, reached a depth of about 350 feet. The depth of the wells in section 31—the westernmost well of the district —is about 1000 feet.

How much farther to the west and north this stratum of oil sand may extend no one knows. Development work is going on in this direction for a distance of 10 or 15 miles. The strata through which the drillers pass along the whole distance is quite similar to that of the present proved oil territory.

Surface Indications

Contrary to the conditions existing in other oil districts, there is nothing on the surface to indicate the immense deposit of oil here found. The surface is hilly with some deep ravines; within the ravines are what is called oil sand, clay and in places shale, but no oil seepages except on the banks of the Kern river before referred to.

The surface, and also the drill, has given evidence that the strata of various kinds are unbroken; that there has been no upheaval of any kind that would dislocate the formation.

The drill has demonstrated that there is a deposit of clay and sand alternating and that there is a third stratum of live oil sand. The depth of the oil sand varies from the 350 feet in the discovery well to 1000 feet on the western limits of the territory. The average depth of oil in paying quantities is about 650 feet.

The Certainty of Finding Oil

On or about September 1st, a report was made after several weeks of examination of the Kern River district and somewhat in detail by a representative of the Bank of Bakersfield. On the date referred to there were 176 paying oil wells completed in this district; there were 112 drilling rigs operating at that time, and it was estimated that by October 1st at least one-half of these wells would be completed. By October 1st, therefore, there would be 232 completed wells in the district within what is known at the proved territory (and consisting of 7,000 to 8,000 acres of land). There never has been a failure to find a paying well, and it is but reasonable to expect that within that area there never will be found a dry hole. It is as morally certain that a paying well will be found in every acre of the territory named as it would be certain to find water in a valley alongside of a river where the fill is sand.

The stratum in which the oil is found is not sand stone, sand rock nor oil sand as it is sometimes called, but sand saturated with oil; the oil percolates through the sand as water percolates through it. This bed of sand saturated with oil is so different from any other formation in California where oil has been discovered that there can be instituted no comparison between the Kern river district and any other oil district known. So many wells have been drilled in the district that it is now known just at what depth the oil will be found and with proper perforations of the pipe about what quantity of oil will be obtained.

Percentage of Oil in Sands

The percentage of saturation of oil in sands of this district has been variously estimated. The percentage of oil in the sands is placed at not less than 10 per cent. and it has been placed as high as 25 per cent.

H. H. Blood, superintendent of the San Joaquin Oil Company and the Sterling Oil Company of this district, and former chemist and assayer of Virginia City, Nevada, is of the opinion that the average saturation of oil in these sands is 15 per cent. In other words, the 400 feet of oil sands such as appear in section 31, 28-28, would be a reservoir of oil covering the whole area under the Sterling property to the depth of 60 feet. If the average percentage of oil is 15 per cent. in the sands and the average depth of oil sand is 300 feet, the average amount of oil over the Kern River district would be 45 feet in depth, providing it were by itself in a reservoir and spread over an area equal to the extent of this district.

Gravity of the Oil

The oil in the Kern River field varies from 12 to 17 degrees gravity; the farther northwest, the lighter the oil and the greater the quantity of gas. It is generally believed that north and west there will yet be developed large flowing wells with oil such as is found in Coalinga, Kreyenhagen, Pico Canyon and other fields where so much is written in another part of this volume regarding the lighter grade of oil.

What the Wells Produce

The wells drilled by what is known as the Santa Fe Railroad Oil Company, but now owned and operated by the Petroleum Development Company and located near the river, consist of about 15 wells; these wells have an average yield daily of 30 barrels. This month the Petroleum Develop-

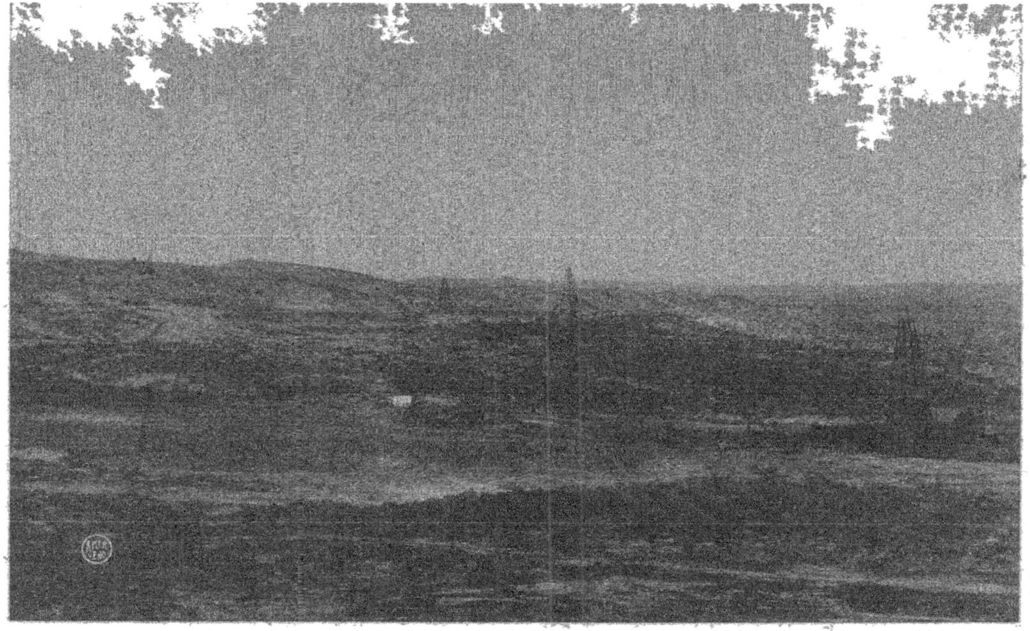

VIEW IN THE MCKITTRICK DISTRICT, KERN COUNTY

ment Company operating these and other wells will ship at least 20,000 barrels of oil. As has been said, the farther west the territory is developed the greater the depth of the sand carrying the oil and as a rule the greater the production of oil from each well.

Some of the wells in section 4, 29-28 yield as much as 300 barrels per day. In section 5, 29-28 still farther west, a yield of at least one of the wells is 250 barrels per day. Other wells in the same section yield as much as 200 barrels per day..

The statement made that the farther west development progresses the greater the yield of the wells must be accepted with some qualifications, and for the reason that the older the wells the less obstruction from the loose sands in the pump and the greater the average daily product. There are four wells owned by the Reed Crude Oil Company in section 28-28, which yield about 125 barrels per day each. In section 31, 28-28, a well owned by the Sterling Oil Company yields an average of 150 barrels. The average yield of the wells in the Kern River district, when in full operation and pumping without any obstruction such as the sand in the casing of a new well, is not less than 60 barrels per day. When all of the 232 wells are ready for pumping and are running without any obstructions, a total yield of the district will not be less that from 12,000 to 15,000 barrels daily.

From present indications, within twelve months from date the Kern River Oil district will be yielding not less than from 20,000 to 25,000 barrels per day.

Probable Duration of the Wells

The estimated yield per acre of oil in the Kern River district by the most prominent oil men of California is not less than 100,000 barrels per acre. Many oil men have estimated the total yield per acre much greater than this. Some have placed the estimate where the oil sand is from 300 to 500 feet in thickness at not less than 200,000 barrels per acre.

Assuming that the average thickness of oil sand in the Los Angeles field is 75 feet, and that the average life of a well is five years, with 300 feet as the average thickness of sand in the Kern River district, the average life of a well there should be twenty years. By analogy the average life of a well in the Kern River district should be even much greater than this, for the percentage of saturation and hence the amount of oil per one hundred feet is very much greater in the Kern River district than in the Los Angeles field or any other oil field yet discovered in California.

Recognizing these conditions, J. B. Treadwell, superintendent of the wells of the Southern Pacific Railroad Company, has stated that the Kern River district within eighteen months will be pumping more oil than all of the rest of the oil fields combined in the State of California.

E. L. Doheny, the well-known oil expert and principal stockholder of the Petroleum Development Company, has made a similar estimate as to the future output of oil from this district.

The Principle Oil Operators

The Reed Crude Oil Company is composed of various bankers and other prominent capitalists of Los Angeles. The Crocker-Woolworth Bank people of San Francisco are operating extensively, having five drilling rigs now in this field, and who control several thousand acres of land. E. L. Doheny, the leading spirit of what was known as the Santa Fe Railroad Oil Company, is giving his best efforts to development work in this field. The Sacramento Oil Company, consisting of some of the Southern Pacific Railroad officials and other prominent capitalists, are also developing oil lands here. J. J. Mack, J. M. Keith and some of their wealthy associates in San Francisco are operating on section 33, 28-28.

W. C. Chapin, Esq., one of the prominent oil operators of Pennsylvania from 1864 to 1876, is now looking over the field with a view of operating here. He regards Kern River oil deposit as the greatest find of fuel oil ever found in the United States.

Dr. W. P. Book, one of the old oil men of Pennsylvania, and W. L. Hardison, of the Los Angeles Herald, but formerly of Pennsylvania; W. D. De Groot, J. Ross Clark, of Los Angeles, and many other well-known capitalists, are also developing their oil lands in this district.

T. Spellacy and other members of the firm of Kerr-Spellacy & Co., of Lima, Ohio, are also giving their attention to the development of oil lands here.

Chanslor & Canfield, who own and control the best lands in the Coalinga oil district, are withdrawing their interests there and investing heavily in the Kern River district, but it is impossible in a short article to give a list of the scores of prominent and well-known oil men that are operating in the Kern River oil fields.

The Continental Oil Company, of Los Angeles, incorporated December 14, 1899; capital stock, 300,000 shares of one dollar each, of which 70,000 remain in the treasury, but are not for sale. Its holdings are as follows: Eight producing wells in the Los Angeles city field; forty acres, patented, in the Fullerton field, adjoining the famous territory of the Columbia Oil Company; one hundred sixty acres in the Ventura field, adjoining the Temescal ranch, recently purchased by a Los Angeles oil syndicate for $500,000; forty acres, patented, in section 29-28-28, Kern River field, on which the company has just completed its well No. 10, which is one of the heaviest producers in the field, and the developments of other companies have demonstrated that every acre of this tract will produce equally good wells. A complete and permanent plant has been erected, two drilling rigs are now at work, and others will be put in operation as rapidly as circumstances will permit. Well No. 11 is down several hundred feet and the company is pushing development with all possible dispatch.

The officers and directors are Wm. F. West, President; Austin D. Elwell, Vice-President; C. E. Price, Secretary; J. Ross Clark and F. W. Burnett.

The Value of Oil Lands

It is most difficult at present writing to place a proper valuation upon the oil lands in this district. C. A. Canfield a few weeks ago, when asked by a newspaper reporter what he considered the value of the proved oil lands in the Kern River district, replied: "In my opinion, $30,000 per acre is a very conservative estimate of the real value of these lands."

The truth reads like a Munchausen tale, or a history of the Pennsylvania oil fields that have produced the Rockefellers of the Atlantic slope.

IN THE SUNSET DISTRICT SHOWING THE JEWETT & BLODGETT WELLS

The stories of sudden wealth acquired on the Yukon in Alaska are tame in comparison with the fabulous wealth developed within the part twelve months in the Kern River oil fields. A prominent capitalist of Los Angeles estimated that proved oil lands here show conclusively that there has been developed at least $200,000,000, on the basis of an average of ten barrels per well for one acre of land. Should the wells average, as it is generally conceded they will, forty barrels per well for one acre of land, the value of the already explored territory would amount to the enormous sum of $800,000,000.

The gold and silver of the Comstock produced wealth amounting to about $500,000,000. The mineral lands of that mining district attracted the attention of the whole civilized world, as will this oil district within the coming two years.

What are the Present Prices of Oil Lands

Proved oil lands vary in price from $3000 to $5000 per acre. Chanslor & Canfield a few days ago refused an offer of $4000 per acre for land in section 29, 28-28. The Secramento Oil Company refused $5000 per acre for their lands in this same section. Lands in section 4, 29-28, in the vicinity of some of the big wells, are not for sale at any price, and it is not probable that $10,000 per acre would be entertained as a purchase price.

Some of the individual wells are producing from 200 barrels to 300 barrels daily, and should be worth at least $50,000 each. As already said, land which produces such an enormous yield of oil as is found in this district can hardly be estimated by the acre, but on the basis of the production of oil.

Leases of Oil Lands

One lease was made by the Kansas City Oil Company of the southwest quarter of the southwest quarter of section 4, 29-28. The royalty in this case was 37½ per cent., the oil to be delivered on board the cars. The Aztec Oil Company also made a lease of the southwest quarter of the northwest quarter of section 4, 29-28, to Mr. James Porteous of the Fresno Agricultural Works, at a royalty of 37½ per cent. of the output, the oil to be delivered on board the cars. There is also a lease on forty acres made by the Stering Oil Company on the northeast quarter of section 31, 28-28, and another lease on the northwest quarter of said section 31, by John M. Bunting. Each lease calls for a royalty of 33 1-3 per cent., the oil to be delivered as in other cases, on board the cars. The option to purchase was placed at the price of $5000 per acre. The Canfield Oil Company has been offered 50 per cent. royalty on a considerable part of their holdings, and the offer has been refused. This will give some idea of the growing demand for oil lands in the Kern River district, and the almost unprecedented royalties offered.

Developments Going On

There are numerous important developments being made in the district; among these there is being constructed by the Southern Pacific Railroad Company into the oil fields twelve to fifteen miles of railroad. The main switch and branch switches will be exceedingly expensive; that part running up the various canyons will cost about $20,000 a mile. In view of the present and future output of oil from this district, the railroad company feels justified in going to this great expense for the purpose of affording facilities for the transportation of oil to the market.

The tankage capacity is also very largely increasing. The San Joaquin Oil and Development Company have recently built three 2000-barrel oil tanks; the same company is now also constructing a tank with a capacity of 37,500 barrels. Chanslor, Canfield & Doheny are just completing two tanks, each with a capacity of 35,000 barrels. The Standard Oil Company also have secured land, and within a few days there will arrive at Bakersfield material for the construction of ten tanks, each having a capacity of 35,000 barrels or a total tankage capacity of 350,000 barrels. There are numerous other similar improvements going on in the district showing the faith of capitalists in the output of oil from this district.

Present Oil Shipments

At present writing there is being shipped daily from this district about twenty-five carloads of oil. So rapid has been the development work that the railroad company has not been in a position to transport all of the product, and hence the output is less than it otherwise would be. It is expected, however, within the next few weeks that the railroad company will afford all the facilities necessary for the transportation of the oil to market.

Cost of Operating

The average total cost of drilling a well, including pipe, in section 4. 29-28, and section 33, 28-28 and various other parts of the district, will not exceed $2500. As the depth increases, likewise does the expense. The wells before referred to are not to exceed 650 to 700 feet in depth. One pumping jack has a capacity of pumping at least twenty-five wells.

Cost of Transportation

One of the most prominent oil men in Kern River district, estimates that the cost of the fuel, the engineers, the wear and tear of the machinery would not, in any event, exceed 1 cent per barrel of the oil produced.

Price of Oil

The present freight rate from Bakersfield to San Francisco, the principal market for oil in California, is 42 cents per barrel. The switch charges from the main track on the S. P. R. R. system into the Kern River oil fields is $5 per car, or about 3½ cents per barrel. This would make a total cost at the present time of 45 cents per barrel for shipping the oil from the wells to San Francisco.

In view of the importance of oil for domestic purposes, in manufacturing and other enterprises, and the immense deposit found, the certainty in finding oil and the comparative small expense in obtaining it, Kern River district is certain to attract as much attention as did the gold fields of Nevada, Placer and Tuolumne counties in

"The days of old,
The days of gold"

in the early history of California.

C. S. YOUNG.

McKITTRICK

Following along the line of the Coast Range from the Sunset district, about thirty-five miles to the northwest, is the McKittrick district, which has its center in township 30 south, range 32 east. The town of McKittrick lies about one-third of the distance between Sunset and Kreyenhagen and a line drawn almost exactly northwest and southeast along the eastern slope of the Coast Range would pass through the oil districts of Coalinga, Kreyenhagen, McKittrick and Sunset. McKittrick was originally known as Asphalto, and the work of developing large beds of asphaltum began here a number of years ago, when the Southern Pacific built a branch road to this point. The asphaltum did not prove profitable and very little was done at that time towards developing oil, although many shallow shafts were sunk, which yielded an average of five barrels of oil per day. Since the recent excitement, however, standard rigs have been put in and there are now a large number of flowing wells. The California Standard, J. B. Treadwell, Milton McWhorter, the El Dorado, and the Giant Oil Company all have good wells. About nine hundred feet seems to be the average depth and the daily capacity of the wells, when first opened, is about two hundred barrels. Some of the wells in this territory have developed large quantities of artesian water. The oil croppings and seepages are very marked and extend in a straight line northwesterly along the slope of the Coast Range towards Coalinga. Standard rigs are being set up at intervals of every few miles and prospecting is proceeding rapidly as far north as the Devil's Den district, where the Spreckels company has recently established a large number of standard rigs and is preparing to exploit for oil. This territory is all quite rich in indications but sufficient time has not elapsed to outline the actual bearing territory.

THE TRUTH ABOUT SUNSET

One of the oldest oil fields in the state and by far the oldest in Kern county is the Sunset district lying about forty miles south and west of the town of Bakersfield. It rests at the base of the first foothills in a northwesterly direction from the Tehachapi mountains and has been prospected for a distance of about ten miles. This extent of probable oil-bearing territory has been known and exploited for the past fifteen years, the pioneer work having been made in the name of the Western Mineral Company under the management of Scofield & Tevis. At the southeeasterly end of the formation, important sulphur beds were developed, from which the natural sulphur has been shipped for several years past. Being encouraged by the developments that had been made by the pioneers Messrs. Jewett and Blodgett, bankers, of Bakersfield, commenced operations about ten years ago and soon found oil carrying about 55 per cent. of asphaltum which has been decided by experts to be the purest asphalt produced in this county. Being so far from the railroad is was necessary to erect a refining plant at the wells and haul only the refined product. This asphalt has found a ready market in the cities of the east at a net profit of about $25 per ton. By successive stages the refining plant has gradually been perfected until it is now one of the most complete and important asphalt plants in the United States.

As additional wells were drilled from time to time, it was found that two grades of oil were to be found in this district. In the oil strike nearest the valley is found the heavy oil, carrying a large per cent. of asphalt. Farther back in the hills, probably a half mile distant, a parallel formation has been discovered which produces a lighter gravity of oil, brownish-green in color and claimed to contain a certain percentage of parraffine. This lighter grade of oil has only recently been found. As a result of the pioneer work of the Western Mineral Company and of the later operations of Jewett and Blodgett, about thirty wells were finished in the Sunset district, the entire product being handled by the refinery on the ground.

Within the past few months there has been a great boom in Sunset and more than a dozen companies are now actively engaged in work with as many more organized and expecting to start operations soon. Among these companies are the State Crude, the Golden Gate, Sunset King, Manhattan, Navajo, Sunset Queen, Sunset District Oil Company, Sunset Czar, Bonita, Sunset Consolidated, Monarch, Los Angeles and Bakersfield, Sunset Petroleum and Refining and others. A majority of these companies have organized through Easton & Eldridge of Los Angeles, who control by lease about 10,000 acres of choice oil land. There are today probably about thirty new rigs in active operation, all of which have been erected since the first of May. The most important new well is that of the Monarch company, which is producing 100 barrels daily. It is located in the north end of the territory as at present exploited. Following the strike of oil by the Monarch company, the Navajo company which is located in the south end of the district struck a fine flow of oil. It is considered certain that the oil belt extends through the intervening territory lying between these two wells, a distance of five miles. Prior to finding oil in these two wells, No. 17 of the Jewett and Blodgett company, lying in the center of the district, was the greatest producer yet discovered. This well has been flowing for the past ninety days at the rate of 150 barrels each 24 hours. Oil is found at varying depths in the Sunset field, running from 150 to 900 feet. The shallow wells, as a rule, produce a heavier oil. Another company which has found abundant oil recently is the Golden Gate whose first well started off as a 100-barrel gusher.

The lack of transportation facilities has been the greatest drawback to the development of the district. This is now about to be remedied, for encouraged by the important developments, the Sunset Railway Company, a Bakersfield corporation, has been organized and and the entire capital of $450,000, required for the construction of a standard-gauge railroad, from Bakersfield to the Sunset district, is now on deposit at Bakersfield. The material is now on the ground and work of construction has begun. Assurances are given that the road will be completed by November, 1900. The road will be operated by the Southern Pacific and Santa Fe.

The district has a good water supply obtained from the hills near by, and the different companies operating in the territory have organized an extensive water system, with a series of artesian wells and an extended pipe line, which will extend about ten miles northwest and southeast, through the district. Lateral lines will be lead to each company's property.

Ventura County

VENTURA county is the mother of oil production in California. Oil was first here produced in paying quantities. For twenty-five years oil has been produced and refined and from present indications the large amount of development work in both old and new bearing sections, the large amount of oil produced in the past is only the beginning of the county's oil industry.

To Mr. George S. Gilbert is given the credit for making the first attempt to utilize the petroleum deposit in the county. In 1861 he put up a small refinery on the Ojai ranch, seven miles from the town of Ventura and a similar institution in Santa Paula canyon, but for a number of reasons the venture was not a financial success and was abandoned the following year, after about 400 barrels had been refined.

In 1864 Leland Stanford and Hayward and other San Francisco capitalists undertook to develop the oil prospects in the seepages along the ridges where these occurred. It was their hope to find a plentiful supply of light oil, familiar to the oil men of Pennsylvania, but in this they were disappointed, for owing to the imperfect appliances at that time, they were unable to drill deep for oil and the tunnels along the ridges, not being deep, of course produced only the heavy black oil. This they considered of very little value in those days, and as the demand was not sufficient, the tunnels were abandoned.

It was in the 60's also that Colonel Thomas Scott of the Pennsylvania Railway Company obtained large land holdings in Ventura county, and through his agent, Thomas R. Bard, now United States Senator from California, began the development of the oil property. Deep wells could not be bored, however, and oil was not found in paying quantities.

Shortly afterwards, Messrs. Adams and Thayer purchased and settled upon land in what is now known as Adams canyon, intending to go into the stock-raising business, but finding oil indications they did some work and shipped oil in small quantities. The gentlemen kept up the work until 1876, when light oil having been discovered in the eastern end of the county, drilling was renewed and a strike was made of the finest light oil yet produced. This well was located higher up on the mountain side and produced about seven barrels a day. Later the Continental Oil and Transportation Company sunk numerous wells and obtained oil. The Pacific Coast Oil Company made the first strike of any importance on their land in the eastern part of the county. In 1876 the Los Angeles Oil Company commenced work near Sespe and made some good strikes. The latter company and the Sespe Oil Company, operating near Sespe, were paying companies in their day. During the past fifteen years numerous other parties have operated in the various fields some financially successful and some unsuccessfully. In 1883 Mr. Lyman Stewart, an experienced oil man of Pennsylvania, came to Ventura county. He was soon followed by W. L.

Graham Photographer

REMARKABLE OIL SEEPAGE ON THE BARD RANCH, VENTURA COUNTY; PROPERTY OF THE BARD OIL AND ASPHALT COMPANY

Hardison, and these two gentlemen formed a partnership known as the Hardison-Stewart Company, and this partnership has done more for the oil industry than any other organization in the state. The company operated on the Pacific Coast Oil Company's land in the eastern end of the county and later in Santa Paula canyon and Adams canyon, on the same land as Adams and Thayer had worked ten years before, Hardison and Stewart put down some wells in Adams canyon which were the deepest west of the Mississippi river. One of them is 2700 and the other 2800 feet deep and both are good oil producers. The Hardison-Stewart Company, Torrey Canyon Oil Company and Sespe Company were finally merged into the Union Oil Company of California, which for years has been the greatest company of its kind in the state, and controls not only the largest and best holdings in Ventura county, but also some of the best properties in Los Angeles, Orange, Kern and Fresno counties.

The oil fields of Ventura county now being operated are: Adams Canyon, Santa Paula Canyon, Sespe, Bardsdale and Torrey Canyon. Torrey Canyon is probably the largest and at present the most productive field in the county.

There have been drilled in Ventura county not less than 425 wells, of which number the Union Oil Company has put down about 300. It is estimated that there are in the county about 200 producing wells at present. There are numerous reasons why the balance of the wells are non-producing. Some are dry roles others were not drilled deep enough, in some tools were lost, while many have been pumped dry. The wells usually start off at the rate of 25 to 125 barrels of oil per day, and within two or three months drop one-half, which flow they hold about a year, and then they continue to decrease until they cease to produce.

The oil-bearing sand is found at various depths in the different localities. There is generally a stratum of shale alternated with a stratum of sand. The hard shale generally carries water, which is not easily shut off. If shale be soft there is no trouble in shutting off the water, when encountered. It is shut off at a depth of from 200 to 900 feet. In all foreign rocks there is always more or less water, which on occasions it is very difficult to shut off. However, where there is no water it is generally necessary to shut off caves. In the Bardsdale territory water is not encountered.

The expense of drilling varies as much as the depth, being from $3000 to $10,000 for each well, according to location, depth and to whether or not water or caves must be shut off. In Torrey canyon the wells run all the way from 700 to 2000 feet deep. The Eureka wells will average about 600 feet in depth and they cost the company an average of $3000 each. In Bardsdale the wells run from 500 to 1600 feet. In the Piru district the wells are 800 to 1600 feet deep. In Adams canyon, the Union Oil Company recently pulled the casing out of the deepest well ever bored west of the Rocky mountains, 3000 feet. They are now preparing to drill 4000 feet in the same locality. In Hopper canyon there are producing wells from 90 to 450 feet deep. In this county there are wells at all depths.

Many of the wells in the county have been phenominal producers. The Union Oil Company has a well in Tar creek over six hundred feet deep, which was sunk in 1893, and started off at 300 barrels a day; it now produces 50 barrels daily. In Adams canyon a well was sunk in 1887 which at the start produced 350 barrels of oil daily. It is now dry, but in less than two years it yielded 125,000 barrels of oil. This is the best well ever struck in the county. The total output in Ventura county is estimated at about 50,000 barrels of oil per month, or 600,000 barrels of oil per annum. The most productive district in the county is the Torrey Canyon territory, which yields daily about 800 barrels.

Like all other matters pertaining to the industry the degree of gravity of the oil varies greatly, ranging from 14 degrees to 32 degrees. The color is usually black or brown but some light-gravity oil has been found with a decided greenish cast. The cost of operating wells is another matter in which there is great variation, but it is believed that fifty cents a barrel would be a fair average.

The transportation problem has been greatly simplified by the building of numerous pipe lines, connecting with the coast and shipping to San Francisco by water. The high freight rates charged by railroads is thus escaped. During the year 1899 nearly a half million barrels were shipped by tank steamers. The Union Oil Company handles a large proportion of the county's oil production at its San Francisco refinery. The Alcatraz Asphalt Works in Santa Barbara county also uses considerable of the output.

There are something like five hundred or more miles of oil pipe line in this county, most of which is controlled by the Union and Pacific Coast Oil companies. The Pacific Coast Oil Company has a two- and three-inch line running from its territory in Pico canyon to Ventura, a distance of about fifty miles. The Union Oil Company has a main four-inch line from a point about eight miles above Santa Paula to Ventura, a distance of twenty-three miles. Numerous two-inch lines run from the fields to this main line. It is in this manner that the oil is piped to Santa Paula, and then shipped by rail, or to Ventura for shipment via steamer. The lines extend to every oil section in the county. The steel tankage of the county amounts to about 137,000 barrels, of which the Union Oil Company has 111,000 and the Pacific Coast Oil Company 26,000 barrels.

The Union Oil Company owns about sixty oil cars. This company has its headquarters at Santa Paula, the center of the oil industry where machine shops are maintained which the Union controls. Thirty men are now employed and an additional force of twenty men will be put to work soon. New machinery is also being installed. All kinds of machinery are manufactured and repaired for use in oil wells. Five strings of tools were shipped last year to the Hawaiian Islands for boring for water. The Union company pays out over $15,000 per month in Santa Paula.

The principal companies operating are as follows: Union Modelo Lomo, Eureka, Sunset, Anita, Fortuna, Sisar Oil and Asphalt, Lewis & Jones, Capital Crude Oil and Asphalt and the Buckhorn Oil and Transportation. There are numerous companies which have just begun operations, among which are Grant Bros., Whidden-Double, Bradley, Palo Solo, Cayteno and the Temescal Oil and Mining. The Ramona Oil Company is commencing development work on a half section of promising territory, which it owns west of Camulos. The Ojai company has begun work in Sulphur mountain and the Erie company in Torrey canyon, north of Fillmore. The Bard Oil Company which has just been organized with a capital stock of $3,000,000 will begin extensive work at once on the ranch of Senator Bard. It is impossible to give a complete list of all of the companies in the county within the limits of this article.

Santa Barbara County

THE only point in Santa Barbara county where oil is as yet produced in large quantities is at Summerland the most unique oil field in the state if not in the world. In other places mining is carried on under the sea but there the shaft has been sunk on land. Here only is found the place where the drill is sunk through the billows of Old Ocean in search of the oily fluid which has the power to still the raging waters of the deep. The field has some peculiarities of its own, which give it a distinct advantage. Added to the cheapness of the work, the fact that the oil may be loaded into steamers directly from the wharf from which it is produced, saves all cost of transportation to the sea-board and add that amount to the profits of the producer.

The town of Summerland is situated beside the ocean on the sides of steep hills. Just before the land jumps off into the sea, with a sheer descent, the hills fall away into a narrow strip, a quarter of a mile wide and three-quarters long. This strip is almost covered with derricks. Over the bluff along the beach there are many wells, and extending out into the ocean, from 400 to 1200 feet, are a number of oil wharves, from which very profitable wells are sunk into the waters of a mill-pond-like cove, where breakers are unknown, and the oily surface of the water shows scarcely a ripple. Every foot of this territory is valuable, for few dry wells have ever disappointed a Summerland investor.

Directly west rises a high hill known as Ortega Hill. It was upon this eminence that Eugene Knapp of Carpinteria found oil some twenty-one or twenty-two years ago. Mr. Knapp was boring for water. Oil was struck, and, disappointed, Knapp gave up prospecting, not realizing the value of his find.

It was in 1895 that the oil interests were started. Boring was at first confined to the top of the bluff between the water and the hills. There was at first a natural gas excitement which grew into a steady development of the oil field. In 1894 the Bourquin brothers dug a hole on the beach in front of the town. They went only six or eight feet, but oil seeped into this pit. The first suggestion of boring into the ocean originated in a paragraph of a State Mining Bureau pamphlet, written by W. L. Watts, and published in 1896. In 1895 H. L. Williams sunk a sucessful well through the sand, and in 1896 S. W. Knapp started the beach rush, which has produced so much oil. His first well was completed on June 1 of that year. Later, J. B. Treadwell built the first oil wharf into the ocean, and proved that there were two oil strata, and that the second one was very profitable. He now has 1200 feet of wharf, and one well is as deep as 850 feet.

The formation at Summerland is composed of sand, beach boulders, clay, shale, sandstone and clay, pitching toward the ocean at an angle of 45 degrees, the strike running southeast and northwest. The majority of the

OIL AND WATER—ONE OF CALIFORNIA'S OIL PHENOMENA, SUMMERLAND, [illegible]

wells are about 250 feet deep. Some run down only 125 feet. There are two oil strata. The first is struck at from 80 to 200 feet, and varies in depth from 25 to 75 feet. The farther into the ocean the well is drilled, the thicker the stratum is found to be. The foundation is clay. Sand and water are invariably found coming from the wells of this stratum. The second stratum not found ashore, is struck from the wharves at from 320 to 350 feet. Here the gravity of the oil is greater, and the wells are completely free from water. Sand makes but very little trouble. The cost of drilling at present is $1 per foot and some drilling has been done at Summerland for as little as 85 cents.

The average yield of the wells cannot be stated with accuracy. Wells run from two barrels up to sixty, but the majority give from four to five barrels per day. New wells from the wharves sometimes run for a day or so after opening as high as eighty or ninety barrels. The oil is forced out with a tremendous gas pressure. These wells then drop from twenty-five to thirty barrels and run at that rate from three to four months. Then, as a rule, they drop again from five to ten barrels and remain at that point. None of the wells at Summerland run too light to be non-paying. There are no non-producing wells. The degree of gravity of the oil varies from 12 to 16.5 degrees. The average is about 14.

The total output of Summerland is 100 cars or 15,000 barrels per month. The profit to the producer is good. The average cost of production is from 20 to 35 cents per barrel, while most of the oil sells at the wells at 90 cents. Nearly all the oil produced goes to Oxnard to the beet sugar factory, under five-year contract, which accounts for the low price. About twenty cars a month go to San Francisco. This oil brings $1 at the wharf.

Of the 330 wells at Summerland those owned along the beach and sunk from wharves are owned as follows: Mrs. H. L. Williams has ten wells. The Acme Oil Company, Titus Duncan, manager, has twelve wells. The Santa Barbara Oil and Mining Company shows twelve wells. S. K. Knapp is its manager. William S. Moore owns nineteen wells. Upon the J. P. Treadwell wharf, 1200 feet long, there are nineteen wells. The Sunset Oil Company, J. C. Hassiner, manager, has twenty-four wells, with 700 feet of wharf. From two wharves, 800 feet in total length, J. C. Lillis has fourteen wells. C. C. Newman, manager of the Oxnard company, looks after thirteen wells and 1000 feet of wharf. The same gentleman is manager of the Sea Cliff company with 400 feet of wharf and sixteen wells. This wharf lies parallel to the shore. The Southern Pacific Oil Company, not the property of the railroad, has twelve wells and two wharves amounting to 700 feet in all. The Duquesne company, T. D. Wood and R. H. Herron, owners, has 800 feet of wharf and nineteen wells. Near the east end of the field is a 250-foot wharf with one unfinished well, the property of Messrs. Churchill and Webber. On the bluff J. F. Miller owns five wells, next to which the railroad has twenty. W. D. Robinson is pumping fifty wells. Loomis & Eaton have five wells and the Eureka Oil Company has two wells and a pumping plant. The Alliance company has four wells. Samuel Wakeman has six wells. The Royal Oil Company owned by Mrs. S. K. Knapp and Mrs. J. C. Hassinger, has four wells. H. E. Packard has nine wells and Messrs. Parsons and Hancock one. Roy Prescott has two wells. The Castle Rock company has three wells and is boring another. J. C. Wilson has thirteen wells and the Sea Side company, managed by J. J. Cooks of San Francisco, has thirty-six wells. H. R. Mueller has five wells.

The Marine Oil Company, who own and control twenty-one lots on the beach and bluff at Summerland (Santa Barbara county), are now steadily pumping oil from thirty-two wells. Another well is drilling at present, and will soon be completed.

Bids are now in for the erection of a wharf one thousand feet in length upon the company's water front, and upon which some twenty rigs will be placed. This will about double the company's present production of oil.

Nearly all of the companies have shore pipe lines. The Duquesne company has 2000 feet of 5-inch pipe, and S. W. Knapp has 1000 feet of gas line and 2000 feet of 2-inch oil line.

In this progressive age when women are invading every branch of business and every profession and where their sphere of influence is as broad as the Universe, it is not remarkable that we should have a women's oil company. Neither is it strange that the company should be a success.

The Women's Pacific Coast Oil Company was organized, launched into business and is being managed exclusively by women. Men have not been barred from the privilege of buying stock in the company, but otherwise the entire enterprise rests with the fairer sex.

The territory owned and controlled by this company comprises 320 acres in the now famous Kern county district; oil producing lots in the Nob Hill tract, Los Angeles property in the celebrated Placeritos canyon, Newhall, within a few hundred feet of the White Oil wells. They also have a lease on lands in the heart of the Summerland district adjoining producing wells. Work on the first well is progressing nicely, and as the boring is comparatively easy, it will not be long before the company expects to have a producing well. They also have a lease on some lands in the Fullerton district.

The company is capitalized for a small amount of $300,000 of which $100,000 is in the treasury. Par value of the stock is $1 per share. From the beginning of the organization the Women's Pacific Coast Oil Company has been a success. It was a success because its affairs have been managed in the most conservative and business-like manner and because the promoters were shrewd enough to secure the cream of the land in the district that they proposed to operate. It was a success because the public was satisfied, after an investigation, that the officers, conscientious, painstaking, honorable individuals, who would handle the affairs of the company with the same care that they would their own personal business. In these days of fake oil companies the Women's Pacific Coast Oil Company stands like a beacon light, pointing the way to legitimate success in oil enterprise.

The officers of the company are: President, Mary Langley; vice-president, Sarah Tomlinson; secretary and treasurer, Donizells Aldrich; attorney, Elizabeth Kenney; depository, Broadway Bank.

DRILLING IN THE OCEAN. VIEW OF THE SUMMERLAND OIL WHARVE

Orange County

THE oil fields of Orange county are all located in what is known as the Fullerton district, by which more or less comprehensive name is meant the range of hills lying between the mouth of Brea canyon and the mouth of Soquel canyon, together with the territory lying farther east, which, although undeveloped as yet, is in similarity of formation to the already proven territory, gives most excellent promise of what the drill will show when it is sunk the proper depth. Throughout the territory, extending almost to the Santa Ana river, outcrops of sand rock are to be found. This field, at least, as far as the mouth of Soquel canyon, is believed to be the same at that found at Puente and Whittier. In fact, although known as several oil fields, and although several different oil strikes have been discovered, it is now considered probable that this range of hills, which rises on the west bank of the San Gabriel river in the southwestern part of Los Angeles and swinging east, slightly south for a distance of 25 miles to the Santa Ana river, contains practically a continuous oil belt, which will some day prove to be among the richest on the continent. One instance of the richness of the territory has already been mentioned in the long life of the wells in the Puente field and the fact that one single well in this district produced 20,000 barrels within a single year. Another valuable point in this connection is found in the fact that in the territory lying at the mouth of Soquel canyon, where are located a number of different companies, all of which are good producers, at least three valuable oil strikes have been found. The oils found by the Santa Fe, Graham-Loftus and Fullerton Consolidated companies are all similar, but there is a difference in the oil found in the wells of the Fullerton Oil and Columbia companies, a short distance farther east. The oil found in these latter wells is of 35 degrees gravity and is pronounced by the refineries to be the finest oil that has ever been produced in quantity in the State.

During the years following the first successful operations of the Puente company a number of attempts were made in what is now the Fullerton field to develop oil, but without success until E. S. Doheny began work about one mile west of the mouth of Soquel canyon. This was in the winter of 1896 and 1897. Having found oil, he sold his lease on several hundred acres of land to the Santa Fe Railway Company, retaining for himself a share of the net proceeds. The first venture was rapidly followed by the Graham-Loftus, the Columbia, Fullerton Consolidated, Fullerton Oil, and Olinda companies, in the order named.

In 1899 operations were extended to Brea canyon, on the west, where heavy oil seepages indicated the possibility of making rich finds. The first locations were disposed of to Dan Murphy and a number of associates, who were operating under the name of the Brea Canyon Company. Their location was considered to be one of the very best in the whole field. All the property in or adjacent to Brea canyon has been leased or sold for oil purposes. Among other companies interested is the great Union Oil Company, which owns nearly all the land lying between the workings of the Brea Canyon and the workings of the Santa Fe company. It is reported that an offer of one million dollars was refused for this property before a single well had been drilled.

An inadequate water supply has from the first been the great drawback of the field, and in fact, to every company that has operated in these hills. The water wells sunk by the Santa Fe and other companies in this district have not been productive. The water found was not of good quality for the boilers. Water for domestic purposes has been hauled from a distance of several miles, since the beginning of work here. Within the past few months, however, a sufficient supply of water has been purchased from the Anaheim Union Water Company, a pumping plant installed at a point on their main irrigation canal about two miles from the wells, and a pipe line laid to the 15,000-barrel reservoir, which the Santa Fe people have constructed at a sufficient elevation to gravitate water to the various properties, including Brea canyon.

The cost of drilling and equipping the average well of from eight to twelve hundred feet in depth, is estimated at from three to six thousand dollars. Of this amount, the casing forms the largest item, varying from $1.25 to $1.50 per foot, according to the size and perforation. Wages are about the same in all the companies, averaging from $1.75 a day for common labor to $5.00 paid to the driller. The combined working force of the companies operating in Soquel and Brea canyons will average about 250 men. Of these, perhaps one-third have families and are living in tents and cottages on the various properties.

In few oil districts are the surface indications more marked than in the Fullerton district. The line of the anticlinal can easily be traced by an almost unbroken line of brea beds, from the mouth of Brea canyon to the mouth of Soquel canyon. From the point of this outcropping the dip seems to be in both directions. Slightly back either way from the crest of the anticlinal is where the best wells are to be found, although some wells are to be found by drilling directly in the brea beds. In Brea canyon the dip of the oil strike is to the south, so far as the wells thus far developed are concerned, but it is known that on the north side of the canyon, the dip is to the north. At the mouth of Soquel canyon the Graham-Loftus and Santa Fe wells are on the north dip and the Fullerton Consolidated wells are on the south dip. The wells of the Fullerton Oil, Columbia and Olinda companies are on the north dip, but on an entirely different strike. In the developments which are going on farther east, the Soquel Canyon company is sinking a well on the north dip. This conformation of the ground makes the territory especially valuable and many of the companies have lands on both dips.

The Columbia Oil Producing Company is in some respects the greatest oil company of the Fullerton district. The heavy production of the wells and the very light gravity of the oil gives the wells a value not possessed by any other company, and this, taken in connection with the large holdings, puts the Columbia Company on a very stable basis. The property of the company consists of 280 acres held in fee simple and 620 acres held on lease. As yet but a very small portion of this has been exploited, but as all the land was carefully selected by the most reliable oil men of the State, it is considered certain that a large portion of the territory is oil land. The company owns four complete drilling rigs, all of which are kept constantly at work. Also, one-half interest in the Franklin Refining Company, of Los Angeles, one of the leading refineries of the city. The Columbia Company is now pumping four wells in the Fullerton district, the daily output being 200 to 300 barrels. The oil is 35 deg. gravity, and is eagerly sought for by the refineries. It brings $1.80 a barrel f. o. b. Los Angeles. The oil-bearing sand rock in the Fullerton district is reported to be the thickest in the world, and all the wells are expected to be long-lived. The officers of this company are among the best-known oil men of California. W. L. Hardison is President; W. B. Scott, Vice-President and Superintendent; Guy L. Hardison, Secretary, and Harry Chandler, Treasurer. The capital stock is $1,000,000, with shares of $1 each.

The Soquel Canyon company was the first of the Fullerton district to be opened and therefore is the first to be considered. The Santa Fe company was the first in the field. It now has 16 producing wells. The company has a fine pumping plant, capable of pumping fifty wells. Two large 180-horse power boilers furnish the power, the fuel used being gas from some of the adjacent wells. The company has four drilling rigs, which are kept constantly at work, and the large territory is expected to furnish many more wells.

The Graham-Loftus company was second in the field and has eight completed wells and two more drilling. To this company belongs the honor of opening the most sensational well in the district. Last December well No. 2 suddenly began flowing at a depth of 1000 feet and for ten days flowed at the rate of 700 barrels a day. Fully 7000 barrels ran into the gulch which was hastily dammed to save the oil. The well is still a fine producer. This company sells its product to the Union Oil Company, it being conveyed to the tanks of that organization at the mouth of Brea canyon by pipe line.

The Fullerton Consolidated Company has two wells pumping and two more drilling. The completed wells are excellent producers and when first opened were gushers, throwing oil at intervals to the top of the derricks. The company will sink a large number of wells.

The Columbia company has four completed wells, which produce oil of 35 degrees gravity. The light gravity makes the oil almost twice as valuable as ordinary oil. The four wells are producing 200 barrels per day. The company is rich in land, owning 280 acres in fee simple and holding 620 acres by lease. The large quantities of gas and the light specific gravity of the oils has made the operations of this company very sensational. One well, when first opened, flowed at the rate of 400 barrels a day for several days, and when deepened, started gushing again. The gas was ignited and several hundred barrels burned beside two derricks. The oil is very volatile and accompanied by large quantities of gas.

The Fullerton Oil Company has two completed wells, which are producing about 100 barrels daily, and will drill ten more on the same strike. The land of this company is crossed by the same stratum found in the Fullerton Consolidated property, but this has not yet been exploited. The light oil which is being produced brings $1.80 a barrel at the well.

VIEW IN FULLERTON FIELD. SHOWING WELLS OF COLUMBIA AND FULLERTON OIL COMPANIES

The Olympic Crude Oil Company has leased the west half of the SE. 1-4 of section 16, township 3 S., range 8 W., eighty acres and is making arrangements to commence work before Oct. 1, 1900. The north and south dip of the Fullerton anticlinal extends directly through from west to east and it is expected that this will prove a very valuable producer. They have joined with the Monarch Crude Oil Company, which has the next 80 acres, and will sink a well near the line. This saves time and keeps more stock in the treasury. The management is of live men and will no doubt make this property a valuable one.

The facilities for transporting the oil from the field are excellent, the Santa Fe railroad having built a spur right into the heart of the field and oil is piped from the various properties directly into the tank cars.

The present output of the Soquel Canyon district is in the neighborhood of 26,000 barrels per month, divided as follows: Santa Fe wells, 7,500; Graham-Loftus, 4,000; Columbia, 6,000; Fullerton Consolidated, 3,000; and Fullerton Oil, 2,000.

At present, oil in this field is worth from $1.00 for the 14-deg. oil, suitable only for fuel, to $1.62 for the high grade oil of 35 deg. or above. The actual cost of production per barrel is variously estimated from 35 cents to 50 cents, depending on the difficulty met with in putting down the well, and in operating it after completed. The Santa Fe company consumes all of its own production as fuel on its various branches in the state, while the Union company ships to San Francisco.

In the Brea Canyon district, the company bearing that name being the first in the field, has accomplished the greatest development. The company owns 200 acres in fee simple and at this writing is finishing its fifth well. The first well of this company was a fine 200-barrel gusher when first started and still produces nearly 100 barrels per day; all subsequent wells are good producers.

The Union Oil Company owns a tract of land extending from one canyon to the other and expects to put down a large number of wells. Operations were begun only a short time since, but the company now has two pumping wells and three more started. A number of other companies are operating in this territory but as yet none have found oil, but all claim to have excellent prospects. In fact, the entire canyon is alive with oil seepages and its future as an oil-producing section is more than promising. The work in Brea canyon is attended with considerable difficulty on account of large quantities of gas and heaving sand, but when these difficulties overcome, the wells are remarkable producers. Two strata of oil sand are found, one at a depth of 500 to 600 feet and one from 1100 to 1200 feet, the latter being much the richer. The oil is from 20 deg. to 30 deg. gravity. All the oil produced in Brea canyon and probably all that will be produced is handled by the Union Oil Company, being pumped into the storage tank at the mouth of the canyon and thence piped to tide water at San Pedro, from whence it goes by barge to San Francisco. The extreme cheapness in this kind of transportation makes the wells far more profitable than in ordinary fields.

Among the many companies operating in the Fullerton field, none has started in a more substantial, business-like manner, and with more flattering prospects than the Carbon Canyon Oil Company. It is now drilling on its 160-acre tract in Carbon and Soquel canyons, which is owned in fee by the company, and fully paid for, as is also its plant there, including one of the heaviest and finest drilling rigs on the Coast, houses, shops, tanks, teams, etc.

The two canyons, traversing this tract, expose some of the finest formations of shale and sand rock that are to be seen anywhere on the Coast, and if indications are to be trusted, the company will strike a marvelously rich flow. The anticlinal, upon which well No. 1 is now drilling, is traceable directly from the rich wells of the Columbia Company, indicating that the oil found here will be of the same high grade and gravity as that produced by the Columbia.

The advantage and conveniences of this location are unusual. Two wagon roads crossing the property, the Olinda spur of the Santa Fe, and the Union pipe line, both only about two miles distant, where oil may be easily gravitated by a short pipe-line, houses, barns, and water wells now on the ground.

While the company is drilling its No. 1 in such a manner as to permit it to go to a depth of 2000 feet or more, if necessary, still it does not place all its dependence on this tract. In addition, it controls 160 acres of patented land in the eastern Fullerton field, adjoining the Scully ranch, to which so much attention is being directed; also 500 acres in the Piru field, close to the Temescal ranch, recently purchased by Los Angeles oil men for $500,000; also 40 acres in the Whittier field, adjoining the Union Oil Co. With five rigs operating within a radius of one mile of this tract, to the east, west and north, it will soon be demonstrated to a certainty, without any expense to this company.

The Carbon Canyon Company is capitalized for $500,000, with the greater part of its stock still in its treasury. Its officers and directors are W. F. West, President; E. G. Judson, First Vice-President; J. R. Greer, Jr., Second Vice-President; C. E. Price, Secretary and General Manager, and F. W. Gregg, G. M. Hawley and J. R. Westbrook.

The following companies are among the recent organizations to enter the Fullerton field: The Fullerton Crude Oil Company is located on the west half of the SW. 1-4 of section 16, township 3, S., range 8 W., eighty acres, and has both the north and south dip of the Fullerton anticlinal. The road is graded and water is being developed and they will commence active operations very soon. The Cortes Crude Oil Company has the adjoining 80 acres on the east, being the E. half of the same 1-4 section. The two companies are joining in sinking the first well so as not to have to put out more treasury stock than necessary. They both have a very conservative management and fine results are expected.

Past experience in the oil business has demonstrated the fact that it requires very large capital to economically develop oil property. With ample capital adverse circumstances can be overcome, and by the law of general average fully taken advantage of, success rescued from the jaws of disaster. Many companies who ventured to develop oil with meager resources are realizing the truth of this as they encounter the inevitable difficulties which attend oil development, especially in untried fields. This has caused experienced men to exercise great caution in regard to providing

VIEW IN FULLERTON FIELD SHOWING WELLS OF SANTA FE, GRAHAM, LOFTUS AND FULLERTON COMPANIES means to carry on enterprises where there are speculative elements, and as far as possible to remove all chances of failure by discounting such chances before the work is begun.

Undoubtedly the oil fields of Southern California are the safest mining enterprises that can be found anywhere. The business is more nearly on the basis of certainty than any other mining industry, and if care is exercised to avoid unnecessary risks, it approximates very nearly, in exemption from risks, to agricultural and business pursuits.

A majority of oil companies rely wholly for success upon the exploitation of one or more pieces of oil territory. If oil is struck the road to success lies open; if not, failure results. This is a necessary sequence of the lack of capital, and should not be regarded as an evidence of bad faith on the part of the management, for the only true test of what lies under the ground is that of the drill. But as more knowledge is acquired of the business, there has been greater inquiry for dividend-paying stocks, and companies which have reached such a stage of development find a ready sale for their shares. With a revenue for paying dividends assured and territory for further development provided, an oil company becomes one of the safest and most profitable opportunities for the investment of capital.

The Northern Consolidated Oil and Mining Company, No. 2, is the last of the Charles Victor Hall dividend-paying oil properties which will be put upon the market. Its shares are of the par value of $1 each, fully paid up, and have been placed upon the market at the price of ten cents each. The company starts out with the ownership of producing oil wells in the Los Angeles oil fields which are now yielding a monthly production sufficient to pay regular dividends, which are expected to continue at the rate of 5 per cent. per month on present price of 10 cents. This secures income upon the money invested from the start.

In addition to this it controls by purchase and leasehold 12,000 acres of rich oil land in the Los Angeles, Fullerton and Coalinga fields, and in Santa Barbara and Ventura counties.

While the nominal capital of the company is $5,000,000, inasmuch as its shares could all be sold at 10 cents, its actual cash capitalization is only $500,000. As a dividend-paying property the wells it owns make the stock worth the money paid for the shares, and as development work progresses upon its other territory, the stock will rise in value until it reaches par. It is an industrial stock, with the probability of ultimate appreciation as the increase in dividends enlarges the net revenue. At the present rate it will pay back the money invested from the present production alone in four years, not counting the value of the casing in the wells and other movable property in connection therewith. Thus, stripping it of all prospective increase in value, it is a good income-paying investment.

The company controls by leasehold, purchase or option the following lands:

No. 1 consists of 7500 acres of oil territory in the Simi rancho in Ventura county, which lies between the famous Ventura county oil fields which align the Santa Clara Valley and the Newhall and Los Angeles fields.

No. 2 is a favorable leasehold upon the Slaughter rancho in San Bernardino county, containing 1160 acres of very rich oil land. This property lies in the eastern extension of the Fullerton field, on the northern slope of the Puente hills, south of Chino. This property has long been regarded as the most promising oil land in that section. It contains deposits of brea, live oil sand, seepages, shale, and other evidences of the presence of oil, and in addition lies in line with the Puente oil wells which have been operated for a quarter of a century, and development now in progress and contemplated will soon bring the property well within a developed field.

No. 3 is a tract of land consisting of 895 acres, known as the Estudillo rancho, situated between Los Angeles and Pasadena. This land lies directly in the tract of the anticlinals connecting the Los Angeles and Whittier fields, and also of the oil strata coming down the San Fernando and San Rafael hills from the west. Development work has been begun within a short distance of the eastern and western boundaries of the tract, which will soon demonstrate its oil-producing capacities. The anticlinals running through this property can be traced for miles, and brea and oil sand is found throughout the tract. Many of the best oil experts have pronounced it excellent oil territory.

No. 4 consists of the Brownsilla, Peyster, Ballard, and Smith ranchos, in Santa Barbara county, near Carpinteria. These properties abut upon the ocean, and in addition to the certainty that they contain oil in large quantities, are underlaid by inexhaustible beds of the finest asphaltum, which can be obtained by simply piercing the overlaying soil for a short distance and elevating it to the surface. The leases cover this in addition to oil. It is one of the most promising properties to be found anywhere.

No. 5. This property consists of 80 acres in section 36, township 2 south, range 9 west. It is located in Carbon Canyon, which branches off from Soquel Canyon to the north, in the Fullerton field. It has several places where the oil sand has been exposed by short tunnels in which large veins of live oil sand have been found. This sand is so rich in petroleum that it will burn when touched with a match, and smells like refined kerosene. On the property is plenty of water for development work, thus saving a heavy item of expense which is often encountered in the Fullerton field. It is in line with the Puente anticlinal, and no better prospects are to be found on the Puente hills than are here exposed.

No. 6 is a leasehold upon 420 acres of oil land in the Sespe Valley in Ventura county, being the Kinney rancho. This land is located in the hills near Sespe, Ventura county, and but a short distance from the wells of the Union Oil Company, back of Santa Paula. The whole district is rich in petroleum and there is more development going on in this district than anywhere west of the mountains and north of Los Angeles county. The Buckhorn district is only a few miles to the southeast, and a well is being drilled within a short distance of the line which gives promise of being a good producer.

No. 7. This is a valuable body of land, containing 1500 acres, about six miles north of Elsinore, in Riverside county. Evidences of oil are found in many places, and in a well 80 feet deep specimens of rich shale have been brought up, which ignite when brought in contact with fire. In addition to the oil right, the leases cover all minerals and clays. The latter have been developed for making tiles, and the section is adjacent to rich gold mines.

No. 8. This is 123 acres of land one mile east of that of No. 7, and is equally as rich oil territory.

The stock of the Northern Consolidated Oil Company, No. 2, has been placed upon the market on terms which will enable shareholders to realize dividends upon the money invested and ultimately be able to dispose of their stock at a large advance over the price paid for it. With such opportunities for development, the stock should advance.

For the guarantee of the Northern Consolidatod Oil and Mining Company, No. 2: If parties now purchasing stock at 10 cents per share shall request the same, the sale will be made on written condition that the stock will, at the option of the purchaser, at the end of one year, be received back and purchase money will be refunded on thirty days' notice, with interest thereon at the rate of 8 per cent. per annum, less dividends paid on same.

San Diego County

A DETERMINED effort is being made to develop oil in San Diego county. About a year ago a syndicate composed of some of her representative citizens sent out several experts to propect for oil, and a thorough examination was made of the territory from Oceanside, a point fifty miles north of San Diego, to the Mexican line, twenty miles on the south. The result of this prospecting has been the securing by purchase and lease of a large acreage which the syndicate believe to be most desirable oil land.

In April last this syndicate purchased from O. J. Stough 700 acres of land at Moreno, a suburb of the city of San Diego, and organized the Monarch Oil Company, and in June commenced drilling. They are now down a little over 900 feet. For the last 200 feet there have been seepages of oil, and from its appearance is light in color and of a high gravity. Gas has commenced showing up, and the company believes that they are very close to the reservoir, and are expecting to strike oil at any moment.

This syndicate also secured a lease of some 1500 ares of land lying between Pacific Beach and the town of La Jolla. This land has been put into the La Jolla Oil Company, and the work on their first well is progressing satisfatorily. They are down about 110 feet, and intend to push the work on this and other wells on the same property as rapidly as it is possibe for them to do so.

Work on these properties has encouraged others and there are now a half dozen companies in the field determined to put down wells. The San Diego County and Victoria Oil companies have been organized to develop lands in the neighborhood of Encinitas, some twenty miles north of the city. The San Diego County Oil Company's well has attained a depth of some 300 feet and drilling will be commenced by the Victoria company shortly. A company has been organized at Oceanside, and they are now drilling, and it is fair to predict that within a very short time the value of this territory will be determined.

Development work here has encouraged others in all parts of the county to prospect, and there have been a number of locations made along the Colorado River; also at Carisso Creek in the Desert county; but in these sections, so far as can be learned, there has been no actual development.

The New York Oil and Improvement Company of Los Angeles, Cal., owning large acreage along the water front at Oceanside, in Los Angeles county, are making preparations to begin drilling on their valuable property.

The experts say that the prospects are equal to those at Summerland, in Santa Barbara county, where large producing wells are found.

Owing to the rush of business at the foundries, the machinery has not yet been received. The company is one of the strongest, and composed of active business men, experienced oil operators, and with unlimited capital.

Dr. James Q. Dixon of New York city, a well-known oil expert with years of experience and excellent commercial ability is president and general manager. Thomas P. Clarke, general manager of the Bonded Attorney's Association of New York, is vice-president. George D. Newham, a prominent business man of Oceanside, California, is secretary.

Among the directors are the following well-known citizens of Los Angeles: H. J. Fleishman, cashier of Farmers and Merchants Bank; Lionel V. Redpath, publisher of "Petroleum in California" and vice-president of the Prudential Mining and Oil Development Company of Los Angeles; H. B. Moore of Arizona, David Ogilvy, civil engineer and architect, Montreal, Canada.

Oil as Fuel in California

THE first and largest use of the crude oil produced in California is for fuel purposes. So general has its use become that at present oil threatens to supersede all other kinds of fuel in the institutions which require great heat or great motive power. It is now the principal fuel on the railrads of the state, in the stationary engines all over Southern California, it furnishes the motive power of the street railways, for almost numberless irrigating plants, the heat for brick kilns, the power in electric lighting institutions and is rapidly making its way into every department of industry in the state. Many steamships and tugs burn oil for fuel in the boilers. The great machine works and iron founderies of San Francisco are arranging to use oil for fuel. And it is not only in great enterprises that oil is making itself felt in the fuel line. It bakes bread and pies in the restuarants and runs the elevators in all the large buildings. The time is near at hand when it will be the fuel used in thousands of cook and heating stoves all over the land.

The method of utilizing the oil for fuel is extremely simple. A small pipe connected with the reservoir of oil is run into the fire-box. of the boiler and connected with a spray from the exhaust steam pipe. The oil and steam thrown off together forms a gas that burns with a steady and intense heat. It is safe, clean, economical, easily handled and expedient. Expert railroad engineers consider it the ideal fuel. The following tests as to the relative fuel value of oil and coal have been taken from a number of different sources and have been amply verified.

The Santa Fe Railroad Company some years ago determined to make a number of practical tests of oil as fuel on locomotives. The relative value of oil and coal for fuel was a matter of the very greatest importance to the company, for if any superiority could be established for oil over coal, it meant that the company would use oil in all its locomotives in Southern California. The tests to be made were to show the relative efficiencies of coal and oil, irrespective of cost. The results of these tests are shown in the official report of the the company and were as follows: Number miles run, per ton of coal, 26.7; number of miles run, per ton of oil, 38.46. By this it was demonstrated that a train could be run 12.39 miles further on one ton of oil than on one ton of coal, showing an efficial power nearly 50 per cent. greater for oil than was shown for coal. Nor did the advantage of oil for use on locomotives cease with its efficiency.

In the matter of cost the advantage was also on the side of oil. Take for instance, the present price of oil—say $1.15 per barrel, delivered—as compared with coal at $7.25 per ton, that being about railroad prices for it. Six barrels of oil, 42 gallons to the barrel and 8 pounds to the gallon, are equal to 2016 pounds, or say one ton of oil, making, at $1.15 a barrel, $6.90 a ton, as against $7.25 a ton for coal. But as a train can be run on one ton of oil 12.39 miles further than on one ton of coal, the cost of oil, mile for mile with coal, is brought down to $4.83 a ton. The results of these tests were sufficient for the Santa Fe Company, and as a consequence oil is used for fuel on all its lines in California, its consumption, now that the line is running its own trains into San Francisco, being more than 2,000 barrels daily. Similar tests made by other railroad companies and manufacturing firms have been productive of equally satisfactory results.

The following in regard to the relative value of coal and Los Angeles oil, as shown by combustion in furnaces, is from a bulletin of the State Mining Bureau by Prof. W. L. Watts:

The heating furnaces of the Los Angeles Steel and Iron Company, one ton Wellington coal equals 2.50 barrels of oil; for steam purposes, one ton Wellington coal equals 3 barrels of oil.

Los Angeles Consolidated Electric Railway Company, steam purposes, one ton of Wellington coal equals 3.62 barrels of oil.

Los Angeles court house, steam purposes, one ton good coal equals 3.10 barrels of oil.

Many other tests have been made and always with the same results. No more severe comparison of the relative cost of oil and coal for fuel purposes can be noted, than that oil which costs $1.00 a barrel at the well in Los Angeles can be shipped to San Francisco at a cost of more than 50 cents a barrel for transportation and sold in competition with northern coal. The steady increase in the use of oil as fuel in all engines, both locomotives and stationary, is ground for the statement that oil is certainly the fuel of the future.

In speaking of the utility of oil as fuel, the Los Angeles Times recently said, after mentioning the question of cheapness: "This is but one of the advantages incident to using petroleum in the place of coal. Engineers say it is much more easily handled, since it can be pumped into the receiving tanks of the tender in a couple of minutes without necessitating any delay, as when coal has to be shoveled into the bins. Oil is safer than coal. There is no possibility of setting out fires along the road, and the expense of clearing a strip along the whole distance of track is thus done away with. Then it gives a steadier fire. The burner is automatic, which practically dispenses with the necessity of a fireman. No cleaning of furnaces is necessary, and the labor about the locomotive is greatly reduced on that account. It requires about an equal amount of room to store a supply of oil as coal, but there is never any loss from dropping the fuel. The pleasure and convenience of travelers is materially increased on a train where oil is used, as there are no flying cinders and ashes, and practically no smoke."

The lighter oils are those that are treated in such a manner as to exclude them from the light, and are calculated for use as illuminants, or as oils for power use in generating power in the so-called distillate engine. While the article supplied by the refineries for use as a generating power is termed distillate, it is, in fact, a refined oil of the highest quality, on which as much labor has been expended as is bestowed on the manufacture of illuminating oil, and as much pains and skill is required to produce a satisfactory gas-engine distillate as is necessary to produce a satisfactory burning oil for domestic purposes.

The advantage that a refinery has on the Pacific coast is the distance from the eastern points or manufacture, and the protection afforded by the long haul across the continent of those products that are manufactured in the east, such as illuminating and lubricating oils. An advantage is also obtained in the manufactture of asphaltum, which is not contained in the eastern petroleum, and for which the world looks to California for the material. Asphaltum is produced, in small quantities only, in Cuba and Egypt, and is produced in large quantities on the island of Trinidad. The Trinidad asphaltum is very widely known, and is well adapted to the laying of asphaltum pavements. It contains upward of 50 per cent. of earth matter, which has to be transported wherever the asphaltum is used. On the other hand, the asphaltum made from the crude oil is better than 99 per cent. pure, which gives it a great advantage over the Trinidad article in the matter of transportation. The asphaltum produced from the refineries is used very largely by parties manufacturing electrical goods as an insulating material, and is used in the manufacture of conduit pipes and for coating iron pipes that are used by the water-works; also in the manufacture of paper pipe. As a roofing material it is unsurpassed, while as a paving material it has no equal.

That California crude oil contains lubricating oils of intrinsic value is beyond question. The business of refining California petroleum now promises to be one of the great industries of the Pacific coast, and parties who take an interest in the business now are bound to reap substantial benefits from their investments, if the works are managed by parties of practical experience.

In a public address made a few months since President Wallace L. Hardison spoke as follows concerning oil as fuel:

"Petroleum, when converted into gas, or when properly burned in liquid form, leaves no soot or dirt, and is free from all smell, leaving no spot or stain upon houses or shrubbery, so that paint remains clean until worn by wind or rain. When the means of burning the various products of petroleum shall have been perfected, and universally introduced, it will be the housekeeper's delight, for then soot and ashes from coal and wood will be a thing of the past. When our streets are all paved and lighted with petroleum products; street cars, motors, locomotives, steamships, factories, machine shops, and other plants are moved by the great force of fuel oil, and our houses and offices are all heated by the same agency to supply the demand will require the development of many times as much territory as is now being operated. Demand and supply will keep pace.

"Perhaps no other one condition has done more to retard the upbuilding of manufacturing and commercial enterprises on this Coast than the lack of cheap fuel. But it has now been demonstrated beyond a doubt that there is an unlimited supply of oil in this State, and in my judgment it is only a question of a short time when capital will seek this locality to establish great manufacturing enterprises, by reason of this cheap fuel found here in such great abundance.

"The development of this great industry at this time is especially opportune. Our recent possessions in the Far East are directing the attention of the whole commercial world to the Pacific Ocean, as never before. Across that great free highway, constructed by the Almighty, reside more than 500,000,000 human beings, now wholly unacquainted with the products of our fields, orchards and factories. Now that we have a foothold at their very door, it will be but a short time before the magic touch of American enterprise will place our products in millions of those distant homes where they were never known before, and I believe that the commerce of the Pacific wil then exceed that of the Atlatic Ocean. When that day comes, as it surely will, no country will receive greater benefits than the United States, and no portion of the United States will receive greater benefits than this Pacific Coast. With cheap fuel added to the rich products of our mines and soil, we are in position at this opportune moment in our national growth to more than hold our own, if we but improve the facilities at our command. Doing this, the day is not far distant when there will be built up here communities surpassing in wealth, comfort and advanced civilization those of any part of the world. Industry is the key to the accomplishment of these beneficial results. and cheap fuel is the greatest motive power of industry."

The leading consumers of oil for fuel purposes outside of the city of San Francisco are here given. A list of the leading consumers in that city was not obtainable, but the total amounts to 100,000 barrels a month. In addition to these amounts it must be remembered that there are hundreds of small consumers. Irrigating plants, laundries, heating apparatus and all manner of institutions requiring heat are using oil, the aggregate being enormous. The consumption by the Santa Fe and Southern Pacific may be slightly large at this writing but will be within the limit in a few months, when the engines now being changed to oil burners are put in use. To this list should be added the consumption of two beet sugar factories, which consume about 100,000 barrels each, during the season of four months.

Santa Fe Railway	60,000
Southern Pacific Railway	45,000
San Diego Water Company	2,000
San Diego Brewing Company	1,000
San Diego Electric Light Company	1,000
National City and Otay Railway	1,000
Redlands Electric Light and Power Company	3,500
Edmond Irrigating Plant (Redlands)	1,000
California Portland Cement Company (Colton)	2,500
Pacific Clay Manufacturing Company (Riverside)	1,000
Santa Ana City Water Works	1,000
Los Angeles City Railway	6,000
Terminal Railway	3,000
Redonda Railway	1,000
Los Angeles Traction Line	5,000
Pasadena Electric Road	2,000
Santa Monica Electric Road	2,000
San Gabriel Electric Company	3,500
Edison Electric Company	3,000
Los Angeles Gas Companies	5,000
Two Los Angeles Breweries	1,500
Los Angeles Brick Kilns	3,000
Ice and Cold Storage Plant	1,500
Cudahy Packing Company	1,500
Simon Maier Storage Plant	1,000
United Electric and Gas Company	1,000
Santa Monica Gas and Power Company	1,000

The Refining of Oil in California

ATTEMPTS were made at refining California crude oil from the earliest discoveries of the fluid. In 1876, when the business of producing oil was practically in its infancy, J. A. Scott, an expert refiner, was sent to the state from Pennsylvania for the purpose of making experiments in refining oil. He was successful to a degree, but for some reason the eastern capitalists failed to follow up the business. Others have taken up the business from time to time, until now there are at least ten refineries in the state. The different gravities of the oil make a diversity in the business of refining and the various institutions range from those which take only the liquid asphaltum to those engaged purely in the business of taking out the gasoline, benzine, kerosene and distillate.

As about all the oil in the state has been produced in Southern California, the refineries have naturally been located in this section, the exception being the Union Oil Company's refinery at Oleum, Contra Costa and the Pacific Coast Oil Company's refinery at Alameda.

Of the refinery of the Puente Oil Company at Chino, mention has been made in the article on the Puente field, and the Jewett and Blodgett plant is described in connection with the Sunset district. With one exception, and that a recent one, all other refineries in the state are located in the city of Los Angeles. The business is rapidly increasing as will be noted from the fact that nearly all the institutions are enlarging their capacity. The Los Angeles refineries are as follows:

The American Oil and Asphalt Company is the parent institution for refining crude oil in the city, although the present company has but lately succeeded to the management. J. A. Fairchild is president and treasurer of the company, E. W. Gilmore, vice-president and general manager; S. Allott, secretary. Heretofore the plant has had a capacity of 725 barrels daily, having three still of 125 barrels each, and two of 150 barrels each. New appliances have just been put in, which increases the daily capacity to 1200 barrels. The company manufactures nothing but asphaltum, of which it turns out 60 tons daily. The plant runs day and night and gives regular employment to a force of about twenty men. The residuum, after the asphalt is taken from the oil, is used for fuel oil and also handled by other refineries, which extract from it the lubricants and illuminating oil.

The Southern Refining Company, which formerly owned the plant of the American Oil and Asphalt Company, has been at work in its new plant for about two months. The plant has a capacity of about 6000 barrels a month and takes from the oil not only the asphaltum, but also makes a fine quality of distillates and engine oils, at present turning out from 200 to 400 tons of asphaltum per month. The plant is new and up-to-date throughout, and is pronounced one of the best oil refineries on the Coast. It uses oil from the Whittier oil fields.

The Asphaltum, Oil and Refining Company, successors to Harris & Frith, is located at Ninth and Santa Fe railroad track. This institution has a capacity of 250 barrels of crude oil daily, and has been running to its fullest capacity. Gasoline, illuminating oil and engine distillates are made of a very superior quality, and all find a ready market in the city. The residuum after the light oils are taken out is sold for fuel oil in car-load lots. The plant has been operation for about fifteen months and has met with such excellent success that its capacity will soon be doubled. The oil used by this company comes from the wells of the Columbia company at Fullerton, and is pronounced by Mr. Scott, the manager, to be the finest oil he has ever seen produced in California in large quantities.

E. D. Roberts is president, H. E. Harris, vice-president; J. B. Frith, secretary. These gentlemen with J. W. Roberts and W. S. Hooper compose the board of directors.

J. A. Scott, the pioneer oil refiner of the State, having come to California in 1876, is superintendent.

The Franklin Refinery Company, of which F. H. Dunham is manager and principal owner, is the successor of the Franklin Lubricating Oil Company. This refinery has been in operation for about four years with excellent success. It is completely equipped and not only manufactures asphalt in large quantities, but all grades of lubricating oil, from a heavy engine oil to the finest grades of bicycle oil. It also makes different grades of distillates. The refinery has a capacity at present of 200 barrels of crude oil daily, but is now engaged in the work of putting in two more stills, which will double the present capacity.

The Union Oil Company at Oleum on the San Francisco bay has a capacity of 600 barrels daily and is kept busy all the time by the numerous wells of this great company. The refined products are handled by the Standard Oil Company and the product sold for fuel. This refinery was formerly located at Santa Paula in Ventura county, where it was operated for about twelve years. About five years ago it was removed to its present location.

The Pacific Coast Company is the pioneer in refining oil in California. The refinery is located at Alameda on San Francisco bay and has a capacity of 1000 barrels a day.

The Hercules Oil Producing Company will have its refinery in operation by November 1st of the present year. The plant will be situated on Santa Fe railroad and Charity street, in the south part of the city near the Franklin Refinery. The Hercules Refinery will have a capacity of 1000 barrels daily and will be the most thorough and complete refinery that has yet been started in California. Franklin H. Dunham, president of the company, is by all odds the most expert refiner of oil on the Pacific Coast and it is by his energy and through his efforts that the Hercules company has been put into existence. The refinery is expected to add new impetus to the local oil industry, and as the company has large interests in oil territory it expects to soon be producing the large portion of the oil needed for the refining works.

Although the process of refining oil is quite simple, many people are unfamiliar with the details, and a brief description of the method will be not only interesting, but profitable.

The first step in the process of refining consists in placing the crude oil in large hollow cylinders termed stills. These stills are enclosed in and supported by heavy brickwork, and are suspended over large furnaces. The heat generated in the furnaces is produced from the combustion of crude oil. The oil in the still is in this way heated above the boiling point, and vapors rise from the surface of the oil and enter large iron pipes that are immersed in water. The vapors, in passing through the pipes, are condensed into a liquid form and emerge from the pipe as distillate.

The whole of the crude oil is composed of various hydro-carbon bodies of varying weight and density, and these different bodies have a different boiling point. In the first process of distilling, these different sections of the oil are separated into their respective series. Those that come off of the still first are lighter in weight and color, and have a low boiling point. As the process of distilling goes on, the boiling point continues to rise, until it requires several hundreds of degrees of heat to lift the vapors out of the still. The products now obtained are crude distillates on the one hand, and the part remaining in the still is refined asphaltum. With some refiners this is all that is done in handling of the crude oil, and the sales are made of the refined asphaltum, and the crude distillates, whose value is only a little above that of the crude oil.

A complete refining plant is equipped with a large number of tanks, in which these various divisions of the oil are stored, and is taken from them separately, and by being excluded from the light and carried through a process of cleansing by the use of sulphuric acid, alkali and water, and again put through the process of distillation for the final separation are made ready for some peculiar use to which they are adapted. Again other portions are exposed to the sun and air and rain and left in open tanks for some time to effect what is called the curing and aging process, which renders them more susceptible to the action of the acids, alkali and water in the purifying process. These oils are finally finished by filtration so as to remove from them anything of a foreign nature that is not an oil perfect in form and color.

Oil in the United States

THE earliest known mention of the existence of oil in this country was made by a French missionary to the Indians in the state of New York in 1627. He wrote of a peculiar oil which was in use among the Indians. It is considered certain that this oil came from a spring near the town of Cuba in Alleghany county, New York. A few references were made by other explorers during that century, and in 1700 the Earl of Belmont, the governor of New York, in his instructions to chief engineer Wolfgany W. Romer, who was setting out on a journey to the western part of the state, said: "You are to go and view a well or spring, which is eight miles beyond the Seneks' fartherest castle, which they have told me blazes into flame when a lighted fire-brand is put into it; you will do well to taste the said water, and give me your opinion thereof and bring with you some of it."

In the year 1783 General Benjamin Lincoln, in a letter to Reverend Joseph Willard, president of the University of Cambridge, says: "In the northern parts of Pennsylvania, there is a creek called Oil Creek, which empties itself into the Alleghany river, issuing from a spring, on the top of which floats an oil similar to what is called barbadoes tar and from which may be collected by one man several gallons in a day. The troops in marching that way halted at the spring, collected the oil and bathed their joints in it. This gave them great relief, and freed them immediately from the rheumatic complaints with which many of them were affected."

In the United States census report on the production, technology and uses of petroleum and its products is an interesting account of the first drilled salt well west of the Alleghanies. It was located on the great Kanawha, a few hundred yards from Camel's creek and not far from Charleston, West Virginia. Work upon it commenced in 1806 and was completed in January, 1808, when a strong vein of salt water was struck at a depth of 58 feet. This effort was followed by other and deeper borings, but in nearly all of the West Virginia salt wells petroleum made its appearance and was a source of considerable annoyance. Some of them were alleged to have yielded from 25 to 50 barrels a day. The petroleum was allowed to flow over from the top of the salt cisterns to the river, where it spread over a large surface and could be traced for many miles down the stream. It was for this cause that the river was nicknamed "Old Greasy" by the Kanawha boatmen.

The first shipment of petroleum in this country was to Pittsburg and is described by Rev. S. J. M. Eaton as follows: "Mr. Cary, one of the first settlers on Oil creek, possessing perhaps a little more enterprise than his neighbors, would collect or purchase a cargo of oil and proceed to Pittsburg and exchange it for commodities needed in his family. This cargo consisted of two five-gallon kegs, that were slung one on each side of a horse and thus conveyed by land a distance of 75 or 80 miles. Sometimes the market in Pittsburg became very dull for a flat-boatman would occasionally introduce a barrel or two at once, that he had brought down on his raft of lumber or logs. At other times the demand fell off so that the purchase of a barrel or two was hazardous." The main use for oil at that time was as a medicine but as yet no one had conceived the idea of utilizing it for light.

The famous "American well," near Burksville, Kentucky, was drilled in 1829 and the following account was published of the phenomenon: "Some months since, in the act of boring for salt water, on the land of Mr. Lemuel Stocton, situated in the county of Cumberland, Kentucky, a vein of pure oil was struck, from which it is almost incredible what quantities of the substance issued. The discharges were by floods at intervals of from two to five minutes each, at each flow vomiting forth many barrels of pure oil. These floods continued for three or four weeks, when they subsided to a constant stream, affording many thousand gallons a day. The oil found its way into the Cumberland river and having been set on fire is said to have burned upon its surface to a distance of more than forty miles below the well."

The history of the oil industry of the country properly begins with the drilling of a well by Colonel Edwin L. Drake on Watson's Flats, below Titusville, Pennsylvania. Oil was found at a depth of 69½ feet on August 28, 1859. Drake was a Connecticut Yankee and his work was done for a company composed of George H. Bissell, J. G. Everlyth, Dr. F. B. Brewer, Jonathan Watson and others. These gentlemen had acquired the land on which the well was drilled five years previously but from various causes had not developed the property. The site of the well was then almost a wilderness, but the existence of oil had long been known and some had been procured from springs. Many delays were experienced before Colonel Drake succeeded in getting his men and machinery in operation. He was at first thwarted by quicksand and water, but he finally drove an iron pipe thirty-six feet down to the rock. This device, said to have been original with Drake, has been of great value in artesian boring ever since he used it. After drilling thirty-three feet, on the 28th of August, 1859, the drill fell suddenly six inches into a crevice, and was left until the next day, when the drill hole was found to be nearly filled with petroleum. No spot in the entire territory where petroleum has since been obtained could have been selected where the oil was to be obtained nearer the surface. The success of this enterprise led to the immediate drilling of other wells; first in the valley of Oil creek and its tributaries, and later over the higher land between Oil creek and the Alleghany river below Tidioute. As this territory began to be exhausted, the region of the Lower Alleghany, in Butler and Clarion counties, yielded wells of great richness, and finally the Bradford field in McKean county became the center of production.

In the early production of petroleum almost all of it came from New York and Pennsylvania. In after years oil was found in eastern Ohio and in West Virginia. Those points at that time were far isolated but so great has been the increase of the fields that they are to all intents and purposes one district, extending from western New York to the Kanawha river in West Virginia.

Prior to 1875 the great bulk of oil produced in the United States came from Pennsylvania and New York, but after that date the production in Ohio and West Virginia and California assumed rapid proportions. The following tables are taken from the reports of the Department of the Interior and embrace all the oil in this country, except where noted. Illinois has produced 5,566 barrels. Missouri, 473 barrels and the Indian Territory 1082 barrels. Wyoming has produced 17,827 barrels. With these exceptions the list is complete. It will be seen that since Colonel Drake drilled the first well the enormous total of 943,513,609 has been produced. This amount of oil would fill a tank with a base of one square mile and one hundred and eighty feet high.

Production of crude petroleum in the United States from 1859 to 1899.

Year.	Pennsylvania New York.	Ohio.	West Virginia.	California.	Indiana.
1859	2,000				
1860	500,000				
1861	2,113,609				
1862	3,056,690				
1863	2,611,309				
1864	2,116,109				
1865	2,497,700				
1866	3,597,700				
1867	3,347,300				
1868	3,646,117				
1869	4,215,000				
1870	5,260,745				
1871	5,205,234				
1872	6,293,194				
1873	9,893,786				
1874	10,926,954				
1875	8,787,514	a200,000	a3,000,000	a175,000	
1876	8,968,906	31,763	125,000	12,000	
1877	13,135,475	29,888	172,000	13,000	
1878	15,163,462	38,179	180,000	15,227	
1879	19,685,176	29,112	180,000	19,858	
1880	26,027,631	38,940	179,000	40,552	
1881	27,376,509	33,767	151,000	99,862	
1882	30,053,500	39,761	128,000	128,636	
1883	23,128,398	47,632	126,000	142,857	
1884	23,772,209	90,081	90,000	262,000	
1885	20,776,041	661,580	91,000	325,000	
1886	25,789,000	1,782,970	102,000	377,145	
1887	22,356,193	5,022,632	145,000	678,572	
1888	16,488,668	10,010,868	119,448	690,333	
1889	21,487,435	12,471,466	544,113	303,220	33,375
1890	28,458,208	16,124,656	492,578	367,360	63,496
1891	33,009,236	17,740,301	2,406,218	323,600	136,634
1892	28,422,377	16,362,921	3,810,086	385,049	698,068
1893	20,314,513	16,249,769	8,445,412	470,179	2,335,293
1894	19,019,990	16,792,154	8,577,624	705,969	3,688,666
1895	19,144,390	19,545,233	8,120,125	1,208,482	4,386,132
1896	20,584,421	23,941,169	10,019,770	1,252,777	4,680,732
1897	19,262,066	21,560,515	13,090,045	1,903,411	4,122,356
1898	15,948,464	18,738,708	13,615,101	2,257,207	3,730,907
Total	572,452,211	197,584,165	73,904,520	12,097,296	23,875,659

a. Including all production prior to 1876.

Year.	Kentucky and Tennessee.	Colorado.	Texas.	Kansas.	United States.
1859	....	....	....	....	2,000
1860	....	....	....	....	500,000
1861	....	....	....	....	2,113,609
1862	....	....	....	....	a3,056,690
1863	....	....	....	....	2,611,309
1864	....	....	....	....	2,116,109
1865	....	....	....	....	2,497,700
1866	....	....	....	....	3,597,700
1867	....	....	....	....	3,347,300
1868	....	....	....	....	3,646,117
1869	....	....	....	....	4,215,000
1870	....	....	....	....	5,260,745
1871	....	....	....	....	5,205,234
1872	....	....	....	....	6,293,194
1873	....	....	....	....	9,893,786
1874	....	....	....	....	10,926,945
1875	....	....	....	....	b12,162,514
1876	....	....	....	....	9,132,669
1877	....	....	....	....	13,350,363
1878	....	....	....	....	15,396,868
1879	....	....	....	....	19,914,146
1880	....	....	....	....	26,286,123
1881	....	....	....	....	27,661,238
1882	c160,933	....	....	....	30,510,830
1883	4,755	....	....	....	23,449,633
1884	4,148	....	....	....	24,218,438
1885	5,164	....	....	....	21,858,785
1886	4,726	....	....	....	28,064,841
1887	4,791	76,295	....	....	28,283,483
1888	5,096	297,612	....	....	27,612,025
1889	5,400	316,476	500	48	35,163,513
1890	6,000	368,842	1,200	54	45,823,572
1891	9,000	665,482	1,400	54	54,292,655
1892	6,500	824,000	....	45	50,509,657
1893	3,000	594,390	18,000	50	48,431,066
1894	1,500	515,746	40,000	60	49,344,516
1895	1,500	438,232	44,430	50	52,892,276
1896	6,005	361,450	113,571	1,450	60,960,361
1897	4,699	384,934	81,098	65,975	60,475,516
1898	24,693	444,383	71,980	546,070	55,364,233
1899*	....	....	....	....	57,070,850
Total	257,910	5,287,842	372,179	613,856	943,513,609

a. In addition to this amount it is estimated that for want of a market some 10,000,000 ran to waste in and prior to 1862 from the Pennsylvania fields; also a large amount from West Virginia and Tennessee.

b. Including all production prior to 1876 in Ohio, West Virginia and California.

c. This includes all the petroleum produced in Kentucky and Tennessee prior to 1883.

*The production for 1899 could not be obtained by states. The figures for the United States as here given are furnished by the Department of the Interior.

Petroleum in Other Countries

Centuries old is the story of the oil industry in foreign countries. From the earliest recorded history we read of the search for and the uses of the "rock oil" or petroleum. Its benefits have been told in fable and song and in some places the oil land was looked upon as sacred ground where the natives and pilgrims were wont to come and worship.

The Russian oil fields stand out boldly by themselves and claim first consideration as they are the greatest oil-producing districts in the world. As early as the tenth century petroleum had become an article of commerce, and was exported by vessels and camels. It was utilized by the surrounding natives for light and fuel. It was in 1773 that Peter the Great issued instructions for extracting the oil and exporting it up the Volga. Prior to 1872 the oil business of Russia had been conducted as a close monopoly, but as soon as it was thrown open to the world the industry assumed vast proportions and enthusiasm was rampant. The gross production of crude petroleum in Russia, at Baku, was 60,597,544 barrels in 1898, as compared with 54,744,303 barrels in 1897, and 49,633,252 barrels in 1896. The increase in 1898 was 5,110,151 barrels. If this production is added to the yield of the Grosni and other districts, which was estimated at 1,800,000 barrels in 1898 and 2,350,000 barrels in 1897, it will make the total production in Russia in round numbers as 62,397,544 barrels in 1898 and 57,100,000 barrels in 1897.

Charles Marvin, an extensive traveler and the author of numerous works treating of the resources and commerce of nations, who in 1883 wrote an account of a journey to the petroleum regions of the Caspian entitled "The Region of the Eternal Fires," says geologically little or nothing is known about the Caspian petroleum region. It has been ascertained that the oil rests in tertiary beds overyling Miocene, but beyond this simple fact science is mute or at fault, and even the engineers working the wells confess themselves ignorant of the conditions regulating the supply of oil. Nearly all of the Russian oil is used for fuel and as it has proven to be a cheap and safe fuel the demand is constantly increasing. The railways of Central and Southern Russia have used oil for their engines for some time and the steamers of the Black and Caspian seas could not be persuaded to use any other fuel except oil. The factories are also beginning to use oil in their furnaces. It is estimated that the railways of Russia consume about 8,000,000 barrels of petroleum per annum. The price last year was about sixty cents per barrel. The entire production of petroleum at Baku comes from a remarkably small area, although geological investigations show that there are over 16,000 acres of probable petroleum-bearing lands, less than 20 per cent. of which has so far been explored. Through the oil industry Baku has been built up from a little, insignificant and unpretentious hamlet into a modern city of thrift and prosperity, with a population nearly equal to that of Los Angeles. At the present time there are over 100 refineries and more are

VIEW IN WHITTIER FIELD SHOWING WELLS OF CENTRAL OIL COMPANY

being constructed. This industry has been of peculiar benefit to Russia not only raising many from poverty to competence and providing work for the unemployed, but it has been a means of increasing its commerce and adding to its financial stability as a nation.

While the discovery of petroleum in Japan is said to date back to 647 B. C., nothing was done to cultivate the lands where petroleum was known to exist until after the discovery of rich deposits in the United States. Before this it had been used for illuminating purposes and for medicine but little or no attention nad been paid to the industry. In 1866 there were fifteen oil districts known in Japan, but it was not until 1875 that the oil production assumed any commercial importance. The oil production in Japan is about 2000 barrels a day. Petroleum is found in all parts of the country but the richest developed fields are in the northern half of the main country. The geological formation is Upper Tertiary, and the oil-bearing rocks are mainly brownish sandstone, loose- and coarse-grained. The depth of the wells is from 300 to 2000 feet.

In India the industry is in its infancy. Several refineries are being operated at Burmah. From the best available statistics the output of petroleum in India in 1897 was 546,538 barrels.

In Italy there are numerous springs of petroleum, and some of them produce petroleum so light that it can be burned in the lamps without refining. For the past six years there has been a steady decline in the pro duction of petroleum in Italy. Yet with the price of $6.84 per barrel every incentive is paid for explorations. But when from this price is deducted $2.25 per barrel excise duty, the situation is materially changed. All minerals in Italy belong to the government, which gives temporary rights to parties wishing to prospect. This fact keeps level-headed men from trying to prospect and thus the industry remains undeveloped, although the indications are most promising.

There was a time when the oil industry was a source of great revenue to Scotland, but in later years there has been little benefit derived from the industry. The American and Russian refineries can furnish illuminating oil so cheaply that it has almost killed the oil industry in Scotland. The number of companies has decreased and the aggregate value of their products seldom exceeds $3,000,000 per annum.

A large amount of capital nas been expended in developing the oil fields of Sumatra, but the results the past year have been far from encouraging. There has been an increase in the yield over the previous year, but all efforts to extend the producing territory have been failures. The older wells rapidly decline and the drilling of new ones is so hampered by government restrictions that it becomes a venturesome business transaction and so capital refuses to invest.

In Java some important strikes were made in 1899 and a pipe line constructed. The production of crude petroleum in Java for 1898 is given at 557,511 barrels.

The Dutch have done some excellent development work in the oil fields of Borneo, bringing this country into favorable consideration, as a petroleum-producing section. The first borings were made in 1897 and at a depth of a little less than two hundred feet a deposit was struck which yielded 440 barrels a day. The Dutch government does not look with favor upon the introduction of foreign capital in its East India possession, but this has not daunted the fervor or the arder with which American capital has been reaching out in that direction. The United States consul at Batavia, in a report to the State Dpartment last year, said:

"The operations I have mentioned cover a very small part of the enormous island of Borneo, and a boundless field for American capital and energy is here offered. Petroleum, coal, marble, precious metals and diamonds have been discovered. Wood and water are plentiful, and the only real difficulties are labor and climate. The former is being solved by importing coolies from China and Java, and as for the climate, one must be as careful as possible and trust to luck. In the interior it is said to be not so bad, and recent developments have shown that most of the tribes of this part of the country are now friendly enough. The native sultans do all they can to encourage enterprise. The Dutch government is inclined to keep out foreigners, but indications are not lacking that it will abandon that policy."

The production of petroleum in Germany while on the increase is still of insignificant proportions, and the output in 1898 was only a little over 500 barrels a day. The oil is of a very dark color and of 28 per cent. Baume gravity.

There is a small amount of oil p duced in Newfoundland. The oil region lies along the west coast, beginning at St. George's Bay and extending a little east of north for 125 miles along the sea coast with a general average width of about ten miles.

Canada produces a small quantity of oil and the industry here was at its heighth at the time petroleum was discovered in Pennsylvania. The industry is of the same age as that of the United States, although oil had been collected from springs and artificial excavations for years before the birth of the "oil fever." The value of the oil produced is about one million dollars per annum. In 1898 10,000 producing wells were reported, with an average daily yield of 2000 barrels. These wells are not controlled by the rich but most of them are in the hands of small owners. Out of the 10,000 wells, 700 different persons are represented in their ownership.

Cuba has rich oil deposits and it is expected that American capital will help in the development of the oil territory. This territory had never been systematically developed but enough work has been done to prove that the ground would yield forth rich results. The oil is very free from water. Near the harbor there are enormous deposits of alphalt, having a thickness of seventy feet. This asphalt brings from $80 to $125 per ton in New York.

Oil has been found in other foreign countries but the development is in many places retarded by governmental hindrances. When the proper inducements are offered for legitimate oil explorations it is confidently expected that the richest finds are yet to be made and that these discoveries will prove that the possibilities of the oil industry is yet in the first letters of the alphabet and that the Omega will not be realized until centuries hence.

Men Who Are Making Oil History in California

WALLACE L. HARDISON

arceau Photo.

Any account purporting to give a story of the oil industry of California, which did not assign a prominent place to Wallace L. Hardison would be very much like the story of Hamlet with the Prince of Denmark left out. For seventeen years his name has been intimately connected with the production of oil in this State, and he is today one of the heaviest holders of oil lands and securities in California. In company with Lyman Stewart, under the firm name of Hardison & Stewart, he was a pioneer oil operator of Ventura county, and through the efforts of these gentlemen the Union Oil Company is today the largest concern of its kind on the coast. Among the other large oil companies which Mr. Hardison has been active in managing and promoting are the Columbia Oil Producing Company, at Fullerton; the Uncle Sam Company, in Los Angeles and Kern River districts; the United Petroleum Company, which controls a majority of the stock of the Union Oil Company, and also has large holdings in the Coalinga fields, and the firm of Hardison & Hardison, which is operating ten wells in the Los Angeles city field. Mr. Hardison has also been active along the line of refining the product of the California wells, and in the early days of Ventura county oil production he was instrumental in erecting a refinery at Santa Paula, which was afterwards moved to Oleum, near San Francisco, by the Union Oil Company. He is a stockholder of the Franlklin Refinery of this city, and treasurer of the new Sunset Refining Company at San Pedro, which has taken a front rank among the refineries of the State.

Mr. Hardison regards his most recent work as one of his best. A few months since he purchased the Los Angeles Herald, and, in connection with a few intimate associates, has given that excellent paper a front rank in California journalism. Through his efforts the Herald is today regarded, not only one of the leading newspapers of the Coast, but the principle exponent of the oil industry of California. The necessity for just such a newspaper has been made apparent by the large measure of success which has crowned the efforts of the new management. As President of the Los Angeles Oil Exchange, Mr. Hardison has contributed in no small degree to the already brilliant career of that young institution. With his large landed interests, his wide and increasing responsibilities, both public and private, the diversified nature of his investments in the oil industry, his large-hearted, open-handed generosity, his disinterested public spirit, unswerving integrity and boundless energy, Wallace L. Hardison today stands as one of the foremost citizens of this great State.

RUFUS H. HERRON

Marceau Photo.

Among the men who from the earliest stages of oil development in Southern California, has devoted his time exclusively to fostering and upbuilding the industry, the name of Rufus H. Herron stands pre-eminent. Coming to California in 1894, directly from the heart of the oil fields of Western Pennsylvania, where for years he had been interested in the production of petroleum, Mr. Herron threw himself heartily into the industry here. With his previous experience he was enabled to act with intelligence and judgment and has been thus more than ordinarily successful.

Mr. Herron is at the head of the largest oil well supply firm found on the Coast, and to his wide experience, intelligent foresight and hearty co-operation with the producers of oil is due the fact that much improved machinery has been introduced into the California fields. His firm was the first to bring to Los Angeles a stock of standard tools such as were used in the oil fields of Pennsylvania and West Virginia. From his beginning in Los Angeles the business has steadily increased until today there are supply houses in San Francisco, Coalinga, Hanford and Bakersfield, the chain of stores forming the strongest and largest house of the kind west of Pittsburgh.

Besides attending to the business of his supply houses, Mr. Herron has interested himself in the production of oil. His experience in the Eastern field educated him in the practical methods of oil production. He is interested in territory in Colusa county in this State, where an excellent quality of lubricating oil is being produced; he is interested in wells in the Coalinga fields, in the Kreyenhagen fields, in the Kern River fields in Kern county, in the Sunset district in that county, and in the Fullerton, Summerland and Los Angeles fields. But these do not claim his immediate attention, he having his representatives, who in the majority of cases are interested with him in the production. By these arrangements his time is not diverted from the business of his supply houses, to which his chief attention is devoted, and which as a result thereof he has made so great a success.

Mr. Herron was instrumental in the organization of the first oil exchange in Los Angeles, and also of the present Los Angeles Oil and Stock Exchange, which has proven to be such a great success. Until the press of his steadily growing business compelled him to resign, he was vice-president and member of the governing board. The name of Mr. Herron is synonymous with sound business integrity, sterling honesty, foresight and good judgment. Thus equipped, it is not strange that he should have made a splendid success in all his business affairs. The oil industry is safe in the hands of such men.

THOMAS HUGHES

an Photo.

WHEN the history of a state or the history of an industry is written, it is but writing the history of the men who have made the state and the industry. The stability of a state or an industry depends upon the stability, intelligence and rectitude of the invividuals. If the oil industry of California, as it now exists, had been builded by only such men as forms the subject of this sketch, it would not be open to the charge of questionable methods, over-capitalization and unscrupulous advertising.

Thomas Hughes has been engaged in the oil business in Southern California almost since the inception of the industry of Los Angeles. To his industry and business sagacity is due the organization and success of a number of the best oil companies in Southern California. He is at present connected with fifteen oil companies and in most of them he is either the manager or an active director.

In company with Edward Strasburg and three others, he first organized the American Oil Company in 1894. This was followed by the O'Donnell Oil Company and others of the most successful oil companies of the city. Later Mr. Hughes was interested in the organization of the Westlake company. Among other companies which he has helped to promote and with which he is still connected are the Oceanic and Alpha in Los Angeles, the Ojai and Bard companies in Ventura county, the Fullerton Oil and Soquel Canyon companies in Orange county, and the Western Union Oil Company in San Luis Obispo county. He was one of the incorporaters of the Oil Storage and Transportation Company, the only organization in the state, formed to buy and store oil in large quantities.

Mr. Hughes has been eminently successful in the oil business. He is exceedingly modest and declares that if any measure of success has attended his efforts it is merely because he has applied common sense business principles to the oil industry. His wide circle of friends and associates declare, however, that he has the judgment to discern, the ability to execute, the firmness of purpose to persevere and the genius to direct. Above all, he has a rugged honesty and probity which gives him the confidence of every man with whom he comes in contact. He is a type of the best in California's citizenship.

FRANKLIN H. DUNHAM

The subject of this sketch comes from sturdy old New England stock, having been born on the shores of Massachusetts Bay. His boyhood days were spent in the midst of a great whaling industry, and from his earliest recollection he was familiar with the process of refining whale oil. From this it was but a step to the business of refining petroleum, and this step Mr. Dunham took while still young. After graduating from the High School he became so deeply interested in the manipulations of oils that he sought a position with the Acme Oil Company at Olean, N. Y., so that he might be able to master all the details of the construction work identical to the business. How well he did this was evidenced by the fact of his being given entire charge of the planning and building of three refining plants on this coast. He developed so marked a talent for business that he was advanced from one place of trust and responsibility to another, until he had a practical knowledge of every department of the work. For quite a period he had charge of testing illuminating oils. In the office of this company he acquired a knowledge of all the details of office routine, and learned the general principles common to nearly all commercial transactions and industrial enterprises. The Acme was a branch of the great Standard Oil Company.

December 28, 1888, Mr. Dunham left the employ of the Standard Oil Company and came to California to accept a position of responsibility with the Hardison and Stewart Oil Company at Santa Paula, his first work being to plan and construct a refining plant for refining their oils.

When the refining plant was afterwards merged into the Union Oil Company and moved to a point near San Francisco, Mr. Dunham had charge of the work of moving and reconstructing the plant. Having successfully set this refinery in motion, he left the Union Oil Company and came to Los Angeles for the purpose of engaging in the refining of petroleum products on his own account. To this end he organized the Franklin Lubricating Oil Company in March, 1897, with a capital of $10,000. The purpose was the production of lubricating oils, distillates and refined asphalts. It was not long before the high grade of these products made more capital and a larger plant necessary. To meet this necessity the name was changed to the Franklin Oil Company and the capital stock of this was $25,000. It was only a year more when another change with a much larger capital was necessary, and the Franklin Refining Company was organized with a capital of $100,000. That was just at the beginning of the present year. Of all these concerns, Mr. Dunham has been and is the president and general manager.

In response to the increasing demand for the refined product, Mr. Dunham, through the Hercules Oil Producing Company, of which he is the organizer and head, is now engaged in building the largest and finest refinery in California. The Hercules Company will soon be a large producer of oil, having excellent territory in several fields. Mr. Dunham has also been active in the organization of a number of local companies, being one of the first to explore the great western field in this city.

It is not easy to say anything in the way of comment which will in any way add to the impression produced by the above plain recital of absolute facts. The facts tell most eloquently the story of a man's career in oil developing, oil refining and in the finding of markets for oil products, which must certainly be called very successful.

"TIM" SPELLACY

"Tim" Spellacy is a character all by himself. There is but one Tim Spellacy in the whole universe. In the oil fields of the East they call him plain 'Tim; in California they sometimes call him Colonel Tim. He is superintendent and general manager of several oil wells, and, according to the custom of the Pacific Coast, as Superintendent in an oil district he is entitled to the distinguished honor of being called "Colonel." He claims to have been born in Conneautville, Pa., on or about July 14, 1854. His friends insist that he first saw the day of light in Ireland, and is a direct lineal descendant of royalty. In business circles he passes for about 46 years of age, but in social life he is still "one of the boys." And a jolly social boy he is. He is an all-round oil man, and tradition says he has been 24 years in the oil business. His elegance as a gentleman now does not seem to smack of his former occupation—that of a tool-dresser. He gives "pointers" in such a way as to confirm the rumor that about 24 years ago, at Edenburg, Pennsylvania, he was a plain, common, ordinary driller. On or about or soon after the introduction of railways into the United States it is said he was known through the oil regions of Pennsylvania, Ohio and West Virginia, and there is little doubt but that this is true, for he had a great reputation as a sprinter. It is recorded of him that he not only distanced John Galloway as a pedestrian, but he waged six days contest among the world-renowned pedestrians in New York City. All this has been reported of him in the California oil fields, and he modestly refuses to deny it. Later he tempted fortune in the vicinity of Dawson and other Alaskan gold fields. Whether as a tool-dresser, driller, or a scout in the Eastern oil fields, judge of a horse race or gold-chaser in Alaska, he has always been the same jolly, good-natured, jovial "Tim" among his fellows. California does not claim him as a native son, but he is now one of us, nevertheless. He reached the Kern River oil fields from Alaska in August, 1899. He is now a California oil man, about as well known as he ever was in the East. He is manager of the California Supply Company, which is owned and controlled by the firm of Kerr, Spellacy & Co., of Bakersfield, whose Eastern office is Lima, Ohio. He is the head of the firm of Spellacy, Woods, Young & Co., operating in the Kern River district, which firm has several producing wells and some of the best territory in that famous oil field. His many years of experience as a practical oil man place him in a position where his advice is sought after and accepted among the leading oil producers of California.

GUY L. HARDISON

Marceau Photo.

Guy L. Hardison was born amidst the active oil developments of Western Pennsylvania, and his life has been spent almost beneath the shadow of an oil derrick. By surroundings, environment, education and inclination he is a thorough and practical oil man, and is today connected with more large petroleum enterprises than any young man in California. Among the large companies with which he has active connection are the following: He is secretary of the United Petroleum Company and of the Columbia Oil Producing Company; he is vice-president of the Imperial Oil Company and assistant treasurer of the Sunset Refining Company and the Globe Asphalt Company; he is a large stockholder and field manager of the Uncle Sam Company, which is operating twelve wells in Los Angeles and has three drilling rigs in the Kern River field. He is manager of the Hardison & Hardison lease, which is pumping ten wells in the Los Angeles city fields. In addition to all these large interests, Mr. Hardison is secretary and vice-president of the Herald Publishing Company, the leading oil paper in California. To all business interests intrusted to his care Mr. Hardison gives the minutest attention in detail and as a consequence all his business affairs are successful. He is connected with a number of large mining enterprises, the principle one of which is the Santo Domingo mine, situated in the district of Carabaya province of Puno, Peru, South America, owned by the Inca Mining Company, whose principal office is at Bradford, Pa., where he spent two years in active mining work. Since returning from South America, he has devoted his attention largely to the oil industry. It is to the pluck, determination, energy, stick-to-itiveness of her young men that the California of the future must look, and among these Guy L. Hardison will always stand pre-eminent.

J. J. O'BRIEN

arceau, Photo.

J. J. O'Brien, the subject of this sketch, is a well known and successful business man of Los Angeles. He has resided in this city nearly eight years, coming here from Kansas City in '92. His first venture in oil was made in '95, and in the old city field, where he operated with considerable success. The low prices for oil, however, following the boom of '96 caused him to dispose of his oil interests and thereafter devote his entire time to the affairs of the O'Brien Investment Company, which he organized in '93 and incorporated in '96, and of which he is president and general manager.

Early in the year '99, it appeared to Mr. O'Brien that the development of the oil-bearing lands of Southern California was to become a great, if not the greatest, industry of the State, he again turned his attention to the production of oil, and about the first of that year obtained a bond for the plant of the Yukon Oil Company, then operating in the Los Angeles field and having an output of more than 5000 barrels of crude oil per month. This property was soon after organized into a stock company in San Francisco and has since paid dividends of about 2 per cent. per month. Following this in December came the Uncle Sam Oil Company, of which he was the chief promoter. This was the first producing oil company to offer its stock on the Los Angeles market, and its success was phenomenal. It has been a large producer from the first, and is today one of the largest producers of crude oil in the local field. This company is now busily engaged in drilling three wells in the Kern River field. Mr. O'Brien is one of the largest stockholders in the Uncle Sam Company, and is also one of its active directors. His latest venture was the organization and promotion of the Lucky Boy Oil Company. This company, too, has met with phenomenal success, having sold in a very short time and with but little effort a large amount of treasury stock, and is now putting up a rig in the Sunset field in Kern county, preparatory to beginning active work. Mr. O'Brien is president and general manager of this company, and is giving largely of his time to its success.

Lucky Boy Oil Company—Board of Directors: J. J. O'Brien, of the Uncle Sam Oil Company; William H. Fuller, Esq., attorney at law; Frank R. Strong, of the firm of Wilde & Strong; Geo. W. Dickinson, of Geo. W. Dickinson & Co., San Diego; Captain Chas. F. O'Brien, Kansas City, Missouri. Officers: J. J. O'Brien, President and General Manager; W. H. Fuller, Esq., Vice-President and Attorney; Frank R. Strong, Secretary; Farmers and Merchants Bank, Depository.

The property of this company consists of the following: First—320 acres of oil land in the so-caled Newhall District; second, 320 acres in the Piru District, and immediately adjoining the famous Temescal ranch. Both these properties are absolutely owned by the company and upon which no royalty will be paid. Third—A lease for 160 acres in the famous Coalinga-Kreyenhagen oil field, which we consider one of the most valuable undeveloped pieces of property in the State.

CHARLES FREDERICK OFF

Marceau Photo.

FEW men in California are more deeply interested in the production of oil than Charles Frederick Off. Although young in years, he has developed remarkable business ability and his name in connection with an oil company gives the organization stability and worth.

Mr. Off was born May 13, 1866, in Louden, Iowa, but while yet a youth of fourteen he moved to Denver, Colorado. After a residence of three years in that city he came to Los Angeles, where he has been ever since. For a number of years he was engaged in the transfer business but when the wonderful oil boom of 1896 struck the city, he decided to devote his time and talents to that great new industry. He is an incorporater and large owner in the Off Crude Oil Company, the Whittier Crude Oil Company, the Pico and Rodeo Oil companies. In connection with H. D. Lombard and A. H Busch, he is now engaged in drilling on the Hollister estate in Ventura county, where the partners have 20,000 acres of promising oil territory under lease. Mr. Off owns and operates several drilling outfits, being one of the most extensive drillers in the field. When the future oil history of the state is written, the list of names of the men who have made oil history will contain that of Charles Frederick Off very close to the head of the list.

List of all Oil Companies Incorporated in California.

The following list of Oil Companies in California is the only complete and authentic one in existence, and has been compiled by the publishers of "Petroleum in California" from the records on file in the Department of State in Sacramento at great expense. The list is copyrighted and cannot be used without permission from the publisher.

Alliance Oil Co., San Francisco, capital, $500,000; par value, $5.00.
Alta Oil & Development Co., Oakland, capital, $500,000; par value, $1.00.
Alpha Land & Oil Co., Hanford, capital, $250,000; par value $1.00.
American Oil & Refining Co., San Francisco, capital, $5,000,000; par value, $10.00.
American Oil & Asphalt Co., Los Angeles, capital, $500,000; par value, $100.00.
American Fuel Oil Co., Los Angeles, capital, $100,000; par value, $1.00.
American Standard Oil Co., San Francisco, capital, $100,000; par value, $1,00.
American Eagle Oil & Mining Co., Los Angeles, capital, $120,000; par value $1.00.
Anita Oil Co., Hueneme, capital $40,000; par value, $25.00.
Anaconda Oil Co., San Francisco, capital, $500,000; par value, $5.00.
Anchor Oil Co., San Francisco, capital $100,000; par value $1.00.
Anglo-Amn. Oil Co., Selma, capital, $375,000; par value, $5.00.
Artesia Oil Co., San Francisco, capital, $100,000; par value, $10.00.
Argonaut Oil Co., San Francisco, capital, $300,000; par value, $1.00.
Arroyo Grande Oil Co., Los Angeles, capital, $500,000, par value, $1.00.
Astral Oil Co., Selma, capital, $300,000; par value, $5.00.
Azusa Oil Co., Los Angeles, $200,000; par value, $1.00.
Acme Oil Co., Los Angeles, capital, $200,000; par value, $1.00.
Alpha Oil Co., Los Angeles, capital, $100,000; par value, $1.00.
Advance Oil Co., Coalinga, capital $250,000, par value, $5.00.
Alamota Oil Co., San Francisco, capital, $250,000, par value, $1.00.
Alert Oil Co., Los Angeles, capital, $500,000; par value, $1.00.
Alexander Oil & Development Co., Visalia, capital, $250,000, par value, $1.00.
Auburn Oil Co., Auburn, capital, $100,000; par value, $1.00.
Aurora Petroleum Co., Fresno, capital, $250,000; par value, $5.00.
Alcalde Oil Co., Coalinga, capital, $445,000; par value, $5.00.
Aztec Oil Co., Bakersfield, capital, $250,000; par value, $1.00.
Anchor Oil Co., Los Angeles, capital, $600,000; par value, $1.00.
Allegany Oil Co., Los Angeles, capital, $350,000, par value, $1.00.
Aroostook Oil Co., Santa Paula, capital, $40,000; par value, $1.00.
Adirondack Oil Co., Fresno, capital, $500,000; par value, $1.00.
Allen & Sutter Petroleum Co., Napa, $6,000,000; par value, $200.00.
Alleghany Petroleum Mining Co., Sacramento, capital, $100,000, par value, $100.00.
Antelope Valley Petroleum Co., San Francisco, capital, $800,000; par value, $100.00.
Antioch Prem. Petroleum Co., Antioch, capital, $1,600.00; par value, $4.00.
Atlas Petroleum Co., San Francisco, capital $5,000,000; par value, $100.00.
Alameda Oil & Gas Co., San Francisco, capital, $100,000; par value $1.00.
American Oil Co., San Francisco, capital $50,000; par value, $10.00.
Asphaltum & Oil Refining Co., Los Angeles, capital, $50,000; par value, $10.00.
Aschner Oil Co., Los Angeles, capital, $40,000; par value, $10.00.
Alcalde Oil & Mineral Association, Los Angeles,
American Oil Paint Co., San Francisco, capital, $50,000; par value, $100.00.
American Crude Oil Co., Los Angeles, capital, $50,000; par value, $100.00.
Allison & Barlow Oil Co., Los Angeles, capital, $10,000; par value, $100.00.
Aetna Petroleum Co., San Francisco, capital, $50,000; par value, $100.00.
Alaska Coal Oil Co., San Francisco, capital, $1,000,000; par value, $10.00.
Anglo-California Oil & Water Co., Fresno, capital, $300,000; par value, $100.00.
Artesia Oil Co., Hanford, capital, $200,000; par value, $10.00.
Avenal Land & Oil Co., San Francisco, capital, $150,000; par value, $100.00.
Arroyo Oil Co., Bakersfield, capital, $250,000; par value, $1.00.
Apolonia Oil & Mining Co., Hanford, capital, $250,000; par value, $1.00.
Anchor Oil Co., Hanford, capital, $150,000; par value, $1.00.
Angel City Oil Co., Los Angeles, capital, $50,000; par value, $1.00.
Argus Mining & Oil Development Co., Whittier, capital, $200,000; par value, $1.00.

Atlanta Oil Co., Bakersfield, capital, $400,000; par value, $1.00.

Alma Oil Co., San Francisco, capital, $400,000; par value, $1.00.

Argonaut Oil & Mining Co., Los Angeles, capital, $600,000; par value, $1.00.

Anchor Oil Co., Visalia, capital, $600,000; par value, $1.00.

Atlas Crude Oil Co., Los Angeles, capital, $300,000; par value, $1.00.

Arena Oil Co., Los Angeles, capital, $400,000; par value, $1.00.

Apex Oil Co., Los Angeles, capital, $750,000; par value, $1.00.

Ashurst Oil Land & Development Co., Stockton, capital, $500,000; par value, $1.00.

Atlas Oil Co., Bakersfield, capital, $150,000. par value, $1.00.

Aetna Oil Co., Riverside, capital, $640,000; par value, $10.00.

Altura Oil & Gas Co., Hanford, capital $100,000; par value, $25.00.

Alta Oil Co., Duniba, capital, $100,000; par value, $10.00.

Alma Oil Co., San Jose, capital, $17,000; par value, $1000.00.

Alcalde Oil Co., Coalinga, capital, $445,000; par value, $5.00.

American Amber Oil Co., Los Angeles, capital, $300,000; par value, $1.00.

Ames Oil Producing Co., San Francisco, capital, $250,000; par value, $1.00.

Barker Ranch Oil Co., San Francisco, capital, $200,000; par value, $1.00.

Bakersfield Fuel & Oil Co., Selma, capital, $16,000; par value, $1000.00.

Bakersfield & Fresno Oil Co., Fresno, capital, $100,000; par value, $10.00.

Bakersfield Oil Co., Los Angeles, capital, $200,000; par value, $1.00.

Bartlett Tutt Oil Co., San Francisco, capital, $100,000; par value, $1.00.

Bay City Oil Co., San Francisco, capital, $500,000; par value, $5.00.

Bachelors Oil Co., San Francisco, capital, $200,000; par value, $1.00.

B. & D. Oil Co., San Francisco, capital, $500,000; par value, $2.00.

Badger Oil Co., Sanger, capital, $100,000; par value, $1.00.

Baltimore Oil Co., Fresno, capital, $100,000; par value, $1.00.

Berry Oil & Development Co., San Francisco, capital, $8,000; par value, $10.00.

Belmont Oil Co., Los Angeles, capital, $200,000; par value, $10.00.

Beaver Oil Co., San Francisco, capital, $100,000; par value, $1.00.

Bear State Oil Co., San Francisco, capital, $200,000; par value, $1.00.

Big Panoche Oil Co., San Francisco, capital, $500,000; par value, $5.00.

Blue Wing Oil Co., San Francisco, capital, $100,000; par value, $1.00.

Blue-field Oil Co., Bakersfield, capital, $100,000; par value, $1.00.

Black Eagle Oil Co., San Francisco, capital, $500,000; par value, $5.00.

Bonanza Oil Co., San Francisco, capital, $150,000; par value, $5.00.

Bonanza Oil Co., Bakersfield, capital, $250,000; par value, $1.00.

Bonanza King of Oil City Corporation, San Francisco, capital, $150,000; par value, $1.00.

Brown Oil Co., Bakersfield, capital, $250,000; par value, $1.00.

Brooklyn Oil Co., Los Angeles, capital, $150,000; par value, $1.00.

Buckhorn Oil & Transportation Co., San Francisco, capital, $200,000; par value, $10,00.

Buckeye Oil & Development Co., Kern, capital, $25,000; par value, $25.00.

Bunker Hill Oil Mining Co., San Francisco, capital, $500,000; par value, $5.00.

British-American Oil Co., Los Angeles, capital, $500,000; par value, $1.00.

Bakersfield Crude Oil Co., San Francisco, capital, $500,000; par value, $1.00.

Barksdale Oil Co., Pomona, capital $200,000; par value, $1.00.

Bedford Oil Co., Los Angeles, capital,$300,000; par value, $1.00.

Brea Canyon Oil Co., Los Angeles, capital, $200,000; par value, $1.00.

Burlington Oil Co., San Francisco, capital, $60,000; par value, $1.00.

Blue Goose Oil Co., Selma, capital, $500,000; par value, $100.00.

Black Diamond Oil Co., Hanford, capital, $32,000; par value, $1.00.

Blue Flame Oil Co. of San Ardo, San Francisco, capital, $500,000; par value, $2.00.

Berkeley Oil Co., Los Angeles, capital, $450,000; par value, $1.00.

Black Goose Oil Co., Bakersfield, capital, $500,000; par value, $1,00

Burbank Crude Oil Co., Burbank, capital, $200,000; par value, $1.00.

Baker Oil & Gypsum Co., Los Angeles, capital, $300,000; par value, $1.00.

Black Jack Oil Co., San Francisco, capital, $100,000; par value, $1.00.

Ben Porter Oil Co., Los Angeles, capital, $600,000; par value, $1.00.

Big Flour Oil Co., Los Angeles, capital, $600,000; par value, $1.00.

Brookdale Oil Co., Los Angeles, capital, $500,000; par value, $1.00.

Bonita Oil Co., San Francisco, capital, $500,000; par value, $2.50.

Black Geyser Oil Co., Los Angeles, capital, $500,000; par value, $1.00.

Banner Oil Co., Los Angeles, capital, $250,000; par value, $2.00.

Bennett Oil Co., San Francisco, capital, $120,000; par value, $100.00.

Bear Creek Petroleum & Mining Co., Bear Valley, capital, $2500.00; par value, $25.00.

Boushey Oil Co., San Francisco, capital, $125,000; par value, $25.00.

Buckeye Petroleum Co., Eureka, capital, $640,000; par value, $500.00.

Buena Vista Petroleum Co., Bear Valley, capital, $1,700,000; par value, $1000.00.

Buckhorn Oil Mining Co., Buckhorn, capital, $12,000; par value, $10.00.

Battle Mountain Gas, Oil & Coal Co., Sutter City, capital, $100,000; par value, $10.00.

Bard Oil & Asphalt Co., Los Angeles, capital, $2,000,000; par value, $1.00.

Belgium-American Oil Mining Co., Hanford, capital, $250,000; par value, $1.00.

Bardsdale Crude Oil Co., Los Angeles capital, $200,000; par value, $1.00.

Black Mountain Petroleum Co., Los Angeles, capital, $200,000; par value, $1.00.

Bradford Oil Co., Fresno, capital, $250,000; par value, $25.00.

Brookins Oil Co., Los Angeles, capital, $20,000; par value, $100.00.

Big Sespe Oil Co., Los Angeles, capital, $600,000; par value, $1.00.

Bouquet Oil Development Co., Los Angeles, capital, $250,000; par value, $1.00.

Bee Hive Oil & Development Co., Oakland, capital, $100,000; par value, $1.00.

Carbon Canyon Oil Co., Los Angeles, capital, $500,000; par value, $1.00.

California Mutual Oil Co., San Francisco, capital, $500,000; par value, $1.00.

Cantua Oil & Development Co., Fresno, capital, $300,000; par value, $1.00.

Caspian Oil Co., San Francisco, capital, $100,000; par value, $10.00.

Callena Oil Co., Selma, capital, $100,000; par value, $5.00.

Casmalia Ranch Oil & Development Co., San Francisco, capital, $50,000; par value, $1.00.

Casitas Oil Co., Ventura, capital, $125,000; par value, $10.00.

Canfield Oil Co., Bakersfield, capital, $500,000; par value, $1.00.

Central Oil & Mineral Co., Fresno, capital, $500,000; par value, 1.00.

Central California Oil Co., Alameda, capital, $100,000; par value,$1.00.

Century Oil Co. of California, Oakland, capital, $100,000; par value; $1.00.

Century Oil & Develpoment Co., San Francisco, capital $400,000; par value, $50.00.

Central California Oil Co. of Coalinga, San Francisco, capital, $250,000; par value, $2.50.

Central Oil Co. of Los Angeles, Los Angeles, capital, $750,000; par value, $1.00.

Central Point Oil Co., Fresno, capital, $100,-000, par value, $1.00.

Chanslor Oil Co., Bakersfield, capital, $500,000; par value, $1.00.

Clam Shell Oil Co., Bakersfield, capital $25,000; par value, $100.00.

Caledonia Oil Land Co., Los Angeles, capital, $600,000; par value, $1.00.

Consolidated Olinda Oil Co., San Francisco, capital, $500,000; par value, $10.00.

Contra Costa Paraffine Oil Co., Oakland, capital, $100,000; par value, $1.00.

Common Sense Oil Co., Bakersfield, capital, $100,000; par value, $1.00.

Columbia Oil Co., Fresno, capital $100,000; par value, $2.00.

Corbett Oil & Development Co., Selma, capital, $1,000,000; par value, $100.00.

Commonwealth Oil Co., Stockton, capital, $100,-000; par value $10.00.

Commonwealth Oil Co., Oakland, capital, $20,-000, par value, $1.00.

Columbia Oil & Development Co., Oakland, capital, $500,000; par value, $1.00.

Conejo Oil Co., Fresno, capital, $100,000; par value, $1.00.

Cosmopolitan Oil Co., San Francisco, capital, $100,000; par value, $1.00.

Columbus Oil Co., San Francisco, capital, $150,-000; par value, $1.00.

Copenhagen Oil Co., Los Angeles, capital, $100,-000; par value, $1.00.

Cove Oil Co., Tulare, capital, $100,000; par value, $1.00.

College Oil Co., Los Angeles, capital, $50,000; par value, $100.00.

Continental Oil Co., Los Angeles, capital, $300,-000; par value, $1.00.

Cottonwood Oil Co., Bakersfield, capital, $50,-000; par value, $1.00.

Commonwealth Oil Co., San Francisco, capital, $100,000; par value, $1.00.

Commercial Traveler Oil Co., Hanford, capital, $200,000; par value, $1.00.

Coalinga-Kreyenhagen Oil Co., Los Angeles, capital, $100,000; par value, $1.00.

Columbia Oil Co., Fresno, capital, $100,000; par value, $2.00.

Contra Costa Oil & Petroleum Co., San Francisco, capital, $500,000; par value, $1.00.

Consolidated Crude Oil Co., Los Angeles, capital, $250,000; par value, $1.00.

Coalinga Fuel Oil & Gas Co., Los Angeles, capital, $640,000; par value, $1.00.

Commercial Oil Co. of Los Angeles, Los Angeles, capital, $100,000; par value, $100.00.

Croesus Oil & Fuel Co., Hanford, capital, $200,-000; par value, $1.00.

Crown Oil Co., Hanford, capital, $300,000; par value, $1.00.

Crown of the Valley Oil Co., Pasadena, capital, $300,000; par value, $10.00.

Cumberland Oil Co., Los Angeles, capital, $50,-000; par value, $5.00.

Cachalot Oil Co., San Francisco, capital, $50,-000; par value, $10.00.

Casanova Oil Co., San Francisco, capital $500,-000, par value, $1.00.

California Standard Oil Co., Los Angeles, capital, $200,000; par value, $1.00.

Cerro-Bonita Oil Co., San Francisco, capital, $175,000; par value, $1.00.

Comet Oil Co., Bakersfield, capital, $200,000; par value, $1.00.

Comstock Oil Co., Bakersfield, capital, $500,000; par value, $1.00.

Chatsworth Oil Co., Chatsworth, capital, $500,-000; par value, $1.00.

Central Point Oil Development Co., Bakersfield, capital, $100,000; par value, $1.00.

Consolidated Oil Stock Co., Los Angeles, capital, $1,000,000; par value, $1.00.

Coalinga Crude Oil Co., Los Angeles, capital, $750,000; par value, $1.00.

Cooke-Helm Consolidated Oil & Petroleum Co., Los Angeles, capital, $500,000; par value, $1.00.

Cahuega Oil Co., Los Angeles, capital, $200,-000; par value, $1.00.

Colonial Oil Co. of Los Angeles, Los Angeles, capital, $500,000; par value, $1.00.

California Consolidated Oil Stock Co., Whittier, capital, $500,000; par value, $1.00.

Calabasas Oil Co., Los Angeles, capital, $500,-000; par value, $1.00.

Coast Range Oil & Development Co., San Francisco, capital, $150,000; par value, $1.00.

Columbia Oil Producing Co., Los Angeles, capital, $1,000,000; par value $1.00.

Climax Oil Co., San Jose, $100,000; par value, $5.00.

Commercial Union Oil Co., Los Angeles, capital, $500,000; par value, $1.00.

Carmelita Oil Co., San Francisco, capital, $1,000,000; par value, $1.00.

Congress Oil & Pipe Line Co., Los Angeles, capital, $500,000; par value, $1.00.

California Petroleum Land Co., Los Angeles, capital, $50,000; par value, $100.00.

Cuyama Valley Oil Co., Los Angeles, capital, $1,000,000 par value, $1.00.

Crescent Oil & Mining Co., Los Angeles, capital, $500,000; par value, $1.00.

Cliff Oil Co., Los Angeles, capital, $300,000; par value, $1.00.

Central Consolidated Oil Co., Los Angeles, capital $500,000; par value, $1.00.

Castiac Co-operative Oil Co., Los Angeles, capital, $500,000; par value, $1.00.

California-Coalinga Oil & Development Co., Stockton, capital, $600,000; par value, $1.00.

Climax Oil Co., Los Angeles, capital, $150,000; par value, $1.00.

Co-operative Oil Co., San Francisco, capital, $100,000; par value, $5.00.

Crow Oil Co., San Francisco, capital, $400,000; par value, $1.00.

California Petroleum Development Co., San Francisco, capital, $500,000; par value, $1.00.

Carpinteria Oil Mining Co., Santa Barbara, capital, $1,000,000; par value, $100.00.

Carmelos Oil Co., Santa Barbara, capital, $250,000; par value, $2.00.

California Crystal Oil Co., San Francisco, capital, $1,000,000; par value, $20.00.

California Oil Co., San Francisco, capital, $1,000,000; par value, $10.00.

Cascade Oil Co., San Francisco, capital, $1,000,-000; par value, $50.00.

Cascade Coal Oil Co., San Francisco, capital, $2,500,000; par value, $10.00.

California Oil Co., Los Angeles, capital, $50,-000; par value, 20.00.

Castica Oil Co., Los Angeles, capital, $100.000; par value, $1.00.

California Petroleum & Asphalt Co., San Francisco, capital, $500,000; par value, $50.00.

California Oil & Gas Development Co., Los Angeles, capital, $100,000; par value, $10.00.

Central California Oil Co., Los Angeles, capital, $2,000,000; par value, $100.00.

Chrysopolis Petroleum Mining Co., Sacramento, capital, $100,000; par value, $100.00.

Chandler Oil Mining Co., Los Angeles, capital, $300,000; par value, $10.00.

Cleveland Oil & Mining Co., Los Angeles, capital, $100,000; par value, $100.00.

Columbia Oil Co., Los Angeles, capital, $200,-000; par value, $1.00.

Califronia Oil Co., Los Angeles, capital, $50,-000; par value, $1.00.

Calumet Oil Co., San Francisco, capital, $500,-000; par value, $10.00.

Caribou Oil Mining Co., San Francisco, capital, $100,000; par value, $1.00.

Central California Oil Co., Selma, capital, $25,000; par value, $100.00.

Cholame Valley Oil Co., Hanford, capital, $200,-000, par value, $100.00.

Columbia Oil Co., Los Angeles, capital, $200,000; par value, $100.00.
Crescent Oil Co., Fresno, capital, $160,000; par value, $10.00.
Caspian Oil Co., Fresno, capital, $100,000; par value, $10.00.
Central Oil Co., San Francisco, capital, $500,000, par value, $5.00.
Crown Hill Oil Co., Los Angeles, capital, $500,000; par value, $10.00.
Coyote Oil Co., Bakersfield capital, $500,000; par value, $1.00.
Commercial Petroleum Co., Fresno, capital, $25,000; par value, $10.00.
Consolidated Oil & Development Co., San Francisco, capital, $50,000; par value, $1.00.
Carbon Hill Oil & Coal Co., Los Angeles, capital, $100,000; par value, $1.00.
California National Gas, Oil & Land Co., San Francisco, capital, $1,000,000; par value, $10.00.
California Oil & Transportation Co., Los Angeles, capital, $25,000; par value, $100.00.
Columbia Petroleum Co., San Francisco, capital, $1,000,000; par value, $10.00.
Combination Oil Co., Los Angeles, capital, $50,000; par value $100.00.
Capitol Crude Oil Co., Los Angeles, capital, $300,000; par value, $100.00.
California Oil Investment Co., San Francisco, capital, $200,000; par value, $10.00.
Capitol Oil Co., Los Angeles, capital, $100,000; par value, $100.00.
Clearfield Oil Co., Santa Paula, capital $50,000; par value, $100.00.
Cosmos Oil Co., Fresno, capital, $100,000; par value, $10.00.
Central Point Consolidated Oil Co., Bakersfield, capital, $200,000; par value, $1.00.
Coast Range Oil Co., Bakersfield, capital, $500,000; par value, $1.00.
Covina Valey Oil Co., Covina, capital $150,000; par value, $1.00.
Crown King Oil Co., Los Angeles, capital, $300,000, par value, $1.00.
Chicago Oil Co., Bakersfield, capital, $300,000; par value, $10.00.
California Oil Prospecting & Developing Co., Los Angeles, capital, $25,000; par value, $1.00.
Caledonia Oil Land Co., Los Angeles, capital, $600,000; par value, $1.00.
Cosmopolitan Oil Co., Los Angeles, capital, $750,000; par value, $1.00.
Concord Oil Land & Developing Co., Sacramento, capital, $100,000; par value, $1.00.
California Sunset Oil Co., Los Angeles, capital, $300,000; par value, $1.00.
California Syndicate Oil & Development Co., Los Angeles, capital, $1,000,000; par value, $1.00.
Dorsey Oil Land & Import. Co., San Francisco, capital, $250,000; par value, $1.00.
Delaware Petroleum Co., San Francisco, capital, $30,000; par value, $1.00.
Del Monte Oil Co., Los Angeles, capital, $15,000; par value, $1.00.
Devil's Den Development Co., Visalia, capital, $125,000; par value, $50.00.
Desert Queen Oil Co., Los Angeles, capital, $300,000; par value, $1.00.
Diamond Star Oil & Development Co., Visalia, capital, $125,000; par value, $50.00.
Dividend Oil Co., Los Angeles, capital, $250,000; par value, $1.00.
Danzig Crude Oil Co., Los Angeles, capital, $750,000; par value, $1.00.
Devil's Den Oil & Gas Co., Hanford, capital, $200,000; par value $1.00.
Delta Oil Co., Fresno, capital, $250,000; par value, $5.00.
Dewey Oil Co., San Farncisco, capital, $100,000; par value, $1.00.
Diamond Oil Co., Los Angeles, capital, $200,000; par value, $100.00.
Devil's Den Consolidated Oil Co., Visalia, capital, $103,000; par value, $1.00.
Dominion Oil Co., San Francisco, capital, $100,000; par value, $1.00.
Directors Oil Co., Los Angeles, capital, $12,000; par value, $1000.00.
Duquesne Oil Co., Santa Barbara, capital, $50,000; par value, $100.00.
Damon Land & Oil Co., San Francisco, capital, $250,000; par value, $1.00.
De Groot Oil Co. Los Angeles, capital, $60,000; par value, $100.00.
Del Sable Oil Co., San Francisco, capital, $250,000; par value, $1.00.
Dixie Oil Co., Visalia, capital, $100,000; par value, $1.00.
Diamond Crude Oil Co., Pomona, capital, $100,000; par value, $1.00.
Diana Oil Co., Visalia, capital, $15,000; par value, $1.00.
Dividend Oil Co., San Francisco, capital, $250,000; par value, $1.00.
Dixie Oil & Development Co., Los Angeles, capital, $200,000; par value, $10.00.
Dos Palos Oil & Development Co., Dos Palos, capital, $500,000; par value, $1.00.
Doheny Oil Co., Bakersfield, capital, $500,000; par value, $1.00.
Dyer Oil Co., San Francisco, capital, $200,000; par value, $1.00.
Dodson Oil Co., San Pedro, capital, $300,000; par value, $1.00.
East Whittier Oil Co., Los Angeles, capital, $250,000; par value, $1.00.
Eagle Oil Co., Los Angeles, capital, $150,000; par value $100.00.
East Side Oil & Gas Co., Visalia, capital, $272,000; par value, $10.00.
Eastern Star Oil Co., Fresno, capital, $200,000; par value, $10.00.
Eagle Oil Co. of Silver Creek, Fresno, capital, $200,000; par value, $1.00.
East Piru Oil Co., Los Angeles, capital, $300,000; par value $1.00.
Elaine Oil Co., Oakdale, capital, $200,000; par value, $1.00.
Elwood Oil Co., Selma, capital, $90,000; par value, $10.00.
Elk Oil Mining Co., San Francisco, capital, $135,000; par value, $1.00.
El Modelo Oil Co., Fresno, capital, $150,000; par value, $5.00.
Emerald Oil & Mining Co., Sanger, capital, $50,000; par value, $1.00.
Emerson Oil Co., Bakersfield, capital, $20,000; par value, $1.00.
Enterprise Oil & Mining Co., Santa Barbara, capital, $100,000; par value, $1.00.
Escondido Oil & Gas Co., Escondido, capital, $50,000; 4500 shares.
Esto Perpetria Consolidated Oil Co., San Francisco, $1,000,000; par value, $1.00.
Eureka Oil Co. of Los Angeles, Los Angeles, capital, $100,000; par value, $1.00.
Eureka Oil & Mineral Co., Fresno, capital, $176,000; par value, $10.00.
Eureka Oil & Gas Co., Hanford, capital, $500,000; par value, $1000.00
Excelsior Oil Co., San Francisco, capital $250,000; par value, $2.50.
Export Oil Co., San Francisco, capital, $100,000; par value, $1.00.
Edison Oil Co., Pasadena, capital, $250,000; par value, $1.00.
Empire Oil & Development Co., Bakersfield, capital, $300,000; par value, $1.00.
Euclid Oil Co., Los Angeles, capital, $350,000; par value, $1.00.
Eagle Oil Co., San Bernardino, capital, $300,000; par value, $1.00.
Echo Oil Co., Hanford, capital, $200,000; par value, $1.00.
Echo Oil Co., Los Angeles, capital $250,000; par value, $1.00.
Euclid Oil Co., Los Angeles, capital, $350,000; par value, $1.00.
Exchange Oil Co., Bakersfield, capital, $150,000;
Electric Oil Co., Bakersfield, capital, $250,000; par value, $1.00.
Empire Oil & Development Co., Bakersfield, capital, $300,000; par value, $1.00.
El Morro Oil Co., Los Angeles, capital, $200,000; par value, $1.00.
Encino Oil Co., Los Angeles, capital, $300,000; par value, $1.00.

Equitable Oil Co., Los Angeles,, capital, $150,-000; par value, $1.00.
Erie Oil Co., Los Angeles, capital, $350,000; par value, $1.00.
Eureka Oil Development Co., Bakersfield, capital. $500,000; par value, $1.00.
El Cojo Oil Co., Los Angeles, capital, $2,000,-000; par value, $1.00
East Side Oil Co., Los Angeles, capital, $300,-000; par value, $1.00.
Enterprise Son Oil Co., Bakersfield, capital, $320,000; par value, $1.00.
Escondido Oil & Development Co., Escondido, capital, $1,000,000; par value, $20.00.
Equitable Oil Co. of Los Angeles, Los Angeles, capital, $150,000; par value, $1.00.
Electric Oil Co., Los Angeles, capital, $50,000; par value, $1.00.
Eureka Sunset Oil Co., Bakersfield, capital, $600,000; par value, $1.00.
Echo Oil Co., Hanford, capital, $200,000; par value, $1.00.
Erie Oil Co., Los Angeles, capital, $350,000; par value, $1.00.
Eleanor Oil Co., Los Angeles, capital, $300,-000; par value, $1.00.
Elk Oil Co., Los Angeles, capital, $500,000; par value, $1.00.
Erie Oil Land & Development Co., San Francisco, capital, $200,000; par value, $1.00.
Echo Oil Co., Los Angeles, capital, $250,000; par value, $1.00.
Encinal Oil Co., Los Angeles, capital, $300,000; par value, $1.00.
Enterprise Land & Oil Co., San Francisco, capital, $200,000; par value, $1.00.
Esperanza Oil & Gas Co., Hanford, capital, $125,000; par value, $100.00.
El Dorado Oil Co., Selma, capital, $100,000; par value, $1.00.
El Toro Oil & Land Co., Lemoore, capital, $100,000; par value, $100.00.
Eureka Consolidated Fuel & Oil Co., Selma, capital, $250,000; par value,, $10.00.
Elite Oil Co., Visalia, capital, $200,000; par value, $5.00.
Excelsior Petroleum & Development Co., San Francisco, capital, $250,000; par value $5.00.
East Fork of Mattole Petroleum Co., Eureka, capital, $400,000; par value, $100.00.
Eagle Oil & Refining Co., San Francisco, capital, $50,000; par value, $100.00.
Eel River Oil Co., San Francisco, capital, $200,-000; par value, $50.00.
Elysian Oil Co., Los Angeles, capital, $1,000,-000; par value, $50.00.
Empire Consolidated Petroleum Co., San Francisco, capital, $2,500,000; par value, $25,00.
Farmers Oil Co., Selma, capital $16,000; par value, $1000.00.
Ferndale Petroleum Oil & Development Co., San Francisco, capital, $100,000; par yalue, $1.00.
Federal Oil Co., San Francisco, capital, $25,-000; par value $10.00.
Fernando Valley Oil Co., Los Angeles, capital, $500,000; par value, $5.00.
Federal Oil & Development Co., San Francisco, capital, $500,000; par value, $5.00.
Fidelity Oil Co., San Francisco, capital, $250,-000; par value, $5.00.
Fidelity Oil Co., San Francisco, capital, $500,-000; par value, $10.00.
Flash Light Oil Co., San Francisco, capital, $200,000; par value, $1.00.
Fountain Oil Co., Oakland, capital, $500,000; par value, $1.00.
Fresno County Oil Co., Selma, capital, $300,-000, par value, $50.00.
Franklin Oil Co., Selma, capital, $100,000; par value, $5.00.
Fresno Oil Tank Mining Co., Fresno, capital, $60,000; par value, $3.00.
Fresno Alpha Oil Co., San Francisco, capital, $100,000; par value, $1.00.
Fresno & Los Angeles Oil Co., Fresno, capital, $250,000; par value, $10.00.
Fountain Head Oil & Mining Co., Bakersfield, capital, $50,000; par value, $10.00.
Fresno & San Benito Oil Co., Fresno, capital, $1,000,000; par value, $5.00.
Fullerton Crude Oil Co., Los Angeles, capital, $100,000; par value, $1.00.
Fullerton Consolidated Oil Co., Los Angeles, capital, $300,000; par value, $1.00.
Fuller Oil Co., San Francisco, capital, $200,-000; par value, $1.00.
4 Oil Co., San Francisco, capital, $300,000; par value, $1.00.
Fossil Oil Mining & Development Co., Merced, capital, $100,000; par value, $1.00.
First National Oil Co., San Francisco. capital, $200,000; par value, $2.00.
Fountain Spring Oil & Development Co., Porterville, capital, $128,000; par value, $1.00.
Franco-California Oil Co., Los Angeles, capital, $400,000; par value, $1.00.
Fountain Oil Co., San Francisco, capital, $200,-000; par value, $2.00.
Fullerton Riverside Oil Co., Fullerton, capital, $500,000; par value, $1.00.
Fountain City Oil So., Merced, capital, $200,-000; par value, $1.00.
Fullerton Home Oil Co., Fullerton, capital, $350,000; par value, $1.00.
Fullerton Crude Oil Co., Los Angeles, capital, $300,000; par value, $1.00.
Fresno Oil Co., Coalinga capital, $500,000;; par value, $5.00.
Freeman & Nelson White Oil Co., Los Angeles, capital, $300,000; par value, $1.00.
Fullerton & Sunset Oil Co., Los Angeles, capital, $360,000; par value, $1.00.
Fullerton Oil Co., Los Angeles, capital, $25,-000; par value, $1.00.
Far West Petroleum Mining Co., Eureka, capital, $200,000; par value $10.00.
Far West Oil Co., Santa Paula, capital, $50,-000; par value, $100.00.
Flowing Well Oil Co., San Francisco, capital, $600,000; par value $100.00.
Forks of the Mattole Oil Co., San Francisco, capital, $1,000,000; par value, $500.00.
Fonner Farm Oil Co., Mattole Valley, capital, $160,000; par value, $100.00.
Fortuna Petroleum Mining Co., Eureka, capital, $30,000; par value, $25.00.
Fortuna Oil Co., Buckhorn, capital, $25,000; par value, $10,00.
Fullerton Oil & Asphalt Co., Los Angeles, capital, $100,000; par value, $100.00.
Fullerton Land & Oil Co., Los Angeles, capital, $1,000,000; par value, $10.00.
Germania Oil Co., Selma, capital, $500,000; par value, $5.00.
Germania Oil Co., Modesto, capital, $100,000; par value, $1.00.
Gilt Edge Oil Tank & Development Co., Fresno, capital, $30,000; par value, $3.00.
Gibbes Oil Co., Stockton, capital, $600,000; par value, $50.00.
Giant Oil Co., San Francisco, capital, $500,000; par value, $1.00.
Gilead Oil Co., Fresno, capital, $100,000; par value, $5.00.
Globe Oil Co., Coalinga, capital, $500,000; par value, $5.00.
Globe Oil Co. of California, San Francisco, capital, $250,000, par value, $1.00.
Gold Oil Co., Bakersfield, capital, $200,000; par value, $1.00.
Gold Nugget Oil Co., Visalia, capital, $200,-000; par value, $5.00.
Golden State Oil Co., San Francisco, capital, $100,000; par value, $1.00.
Golden Gate Oil Producing Co., Stockton, capital, $100,000; par value, $1.00.
Golden State Oil Mining & Development Co., Visalia, capital, $250,000; par value, $10.00.
Golden Gate Oil & Development Co., San Francisco, capital, $250,000; par value, $5.00.
Gould Oil Co. of California, Oakland, capital, $100,000; par value, $1.00.
Good Luck Oil Co., Long Beach, capital, $15,-
Great Western Oil & Develeopment Co., San 000; par value, $10.00.
Grace Oil Co., Bakersfield, capital, $250,000; par value, $1.00.

Great Western Oil & Development Co., San Francisco, capital, $500,000; par value, $1.00.
Grey Eagle Oil Co., San Francisco, capital, $250,000; par value, $2.50.
Grayson Oil & Land Co., Modesto, capital, $250,000; par value, $1.00.
Gypsey Queen Oil Co., San Francisco, capital, $200,000; par value, $1.00.
Garcia Petroleum Oil Co., San Francisco, capital, $400,000; par value, $100.00.
Gumda Oil Co., San Francisco, capital, $20,000; par value, $100.00.
Golden Gate Oil Co., San Francisco, capital, $500,000; par value, $1.00.
Golden Rule Oil Co., Los Angeles, capital, $500,000; par value, $1.00.
Great Western Oil Co., Bakersfield, capital, $500,000; par value, $1.00.
Good Luck Oil Development Co., Long Beach, capital, $200,000; par value, $1.00.
Gas & Oil Development Co., Merced, capital, $1,000,000; par value, $10.00.
Golden West Oil Co., Los Angeles, capital, $280,000; par value, $1.00.
Gonzales Mexican Oil Co., San Francisco, capital, $100,000; par value, $1.00.
Gregory Oil Co., Los Angeles, capital, $300,000; par value, $100.00.
Graves Oil Co., Los Angeles, capital, $250,000; par value, $1.00.
Gunboat Oil Co., Los Angeles, capital, $250,000; par value, $1.00.
Gibraltar Oil Co., Los Angeles, capital, $300,000; par value, $1.00.
Great Northern Oil Co., Oakland, capital, $250,000; par value, $1.00.
Green Mountain Oil Co., Los Angeles, capital, $500,000; par value, $1.00.
Grand Central Oil Co., Los Angeles, capital, $770,000; par value, $1.00.
Grand Central Oil Development Co., Bakersfield, capital, $200,000; par value, $1.00.
Gilroy Oil & Development Co., San Francisco, capital, $300,000; par value, $1.00.
Gem Oil Co., Merced, capital, $200,000, par value, $1.00.
Globe R. E. Oil & Development Co., Los Angeles, capital, $30,000; par value, $1.00.
Great Western Oil Co., San Francisco, capital, $1,000,000; par value, $10.00.
Grocers' Oil Co., Fresno, capital, $100,000; par value, $1.00.
Golden Gate Petroleum Co., San Francisco, capital, $1,000,000; par value, $10.00.
Gloria Mundi Oil Co., Selma, capital, $500,000; par value, $5.00.
Goodenough Oil Co., Los Angeles, capital, $500,000; par value, $1.00.
Golden Gate Oil Co., Los Angeles, capital, $600,000; par value, $1.00.
Golden West Crude Oil Co., Los Angeles, capital, $350,000; par value, $1.00.
Green Whittier Oil Co., Los Angeles, capital, $1,000,000; par value, $1.00.
Grant Oil Co., Oakland, capital, $150,000; par value, $1.00.
Gorman Oil Co., Los Angeles, capital $1,000,000; par value, $1.00.
Gold State Oil Co., Fresno, capital, $500,000; par value, $100.00.
Hanford Cholame Oil Co., Hanford, capital, $250,000; par value, $1.00.
Halcyon Oil Co., Los Angeles, capital, $100,000; par value, $1.00.
Hawkeye Oil Co., Selma, capital, $200,000; par value, $100.00.
Herron Hill Oil Co., Los Angeles, capital, $100,000; par value, $100.00.
Herron Oil Co., Los Angeles capital, $100,000; par value, $1.00.
Herculean Consolidated Oil & Mining Co., San Francisco, capital, $800,266.00; par value, $1.00.
Hercules Oil Co., San Francisco, capital, $100,000; par value, $1.00.
Homestake Oil Co., Los Angeles, capital, $200,000; par value, $5.00.
Holland Oil Co., Hanford, capital, $320,000; par value, $1.00.
Hubbell Oil Co., Los Angeles, capital, $200,000; par value, $100.00.
Hicks Oil Co., Visalia, capital, capital, $250,000; par value, $10.00.
Haley Petroleum Co., San Francisco, capital, $280,000; par value, $100.00.
Half Moon Bay Oil Co., San Francisco, capital, $1,000,000; par value, $10.00.
Hayward Petroleum Co., San Francisco, capital, $512,000; par value, $100.00.
Hawley Farm Oil Co., San Francisco, capital, 750,000; par value, $500,00.
Hardison & Stewart Oil Co., Santa Paula, capital, $1,000,000; par value, $100.00.
Howard & Martin Petroleum Co., San Francisco, capital, $1,000,000; par value, $500.00.
Humbolt Oil Co., Eureka, capital, $1,000,000; par value, $1.00.
Hercules Oil Producing Co., Los Angeles, capital, $600,000; par value, $1.00.
Hamiltonian Oil Co., Hollister, capital, $500,000, par value, $1.00.
Hanford-Fresno-Kern River Oil Co., Hanford, capital, $150,000; par value, $1.00.
Humboldt Oil Co., San Francisco, capital, $20,000; par value, $1.00.
Hope Oil Co., Hanford, capital, $100,000; par value, $1.00.
Home Mutual Oil Co., Sanger, capital, $900.00; par value, $100.00.
Hopper Canyon Oil Co., Los Angeles, capital $500,000; par value, $1.00.
Homestead Oil Co., Pasadena, capital, $500,000; par value, $1.00.
Homestake Crude Oil Ci., Los Angeles, capital, $250,000; par value, $1.00.
Hecla Oil Co., Los Angeles, capital, $500,000; par value, $1.00.
Hiawatha Oil Co., Los Angeles, capital, $600,000; par value, $1.00.
Hopland Oil Development Co., San Francisco, capital, $100,000; par value, $1.00.
Highland Oil Co., Fresno, capital, $200,000; par value, $10.00.
Hanford Oil Co., Hanford, $00,000; par value, $10.00.
Hanford & Oleander Oil & Mineral Co., Hanford, capital, $320,000; par value, $5,00.
Home Oil Co., Whittier capital, $100,000; par value, $1.00.
Home Oil Co., San Francisco, capital $100,000; par value, $1.00.
Ibex Oil Co., San Francisco, capital, $100,000; par value, $1.00.
Imperial Oil & Development Co., San Francisco, capital, $1,000,000; par value, $1.00.
Ideal Oil Co., Fresno, capital, $250,000; par value, $5.00.
Illinois Oil & Asphalt Co., Santa Barbara, capital, $50,000; par value, $1.00.
Imperial Oil Co., Bakersfield, capital, $500,000; par value, $5.00.
Imperial Consolidated Oil Co., Los Angeles, capital, $1,000,000; par value, $1.00.
Investment Oil Co. of San Francisco, San Francisco, capital, $500,000; par value, $5.00.
Independence Oil Co., San Francisco, capital, $600,000; par value, $1.00.
Ingomar Petroleum Co., San Francisco, capital, 250,000; par value, $2.50.
Indian Valley Oil & Land Co., Modesto, capital, $200,000; par value, $1.00.
Interior Oil Development Co., Bakersfield, capital, $100,000; par value, $1.00.
Iowa Oil Co., Hanford, capital, $300,000; par value, $1.00.
Isis Oil Co., Selma, capital, $500,000; par value, $5.00.
I X L Oil Co., Bakersfield, capital, $100,000; par value, $1.00.
Independent Oil & Development Co., Fresno, capital, $100,000; par value, 50 cents.
Imperial Oil Co., Los Angeles, capital, $25,000; par value, $100.00.
Inferno Oil Co., Ventura, capital, $500,000; par value, $1.00.
Ivanhoe Oil Co., Los Angeles, $200,000; par value, $1.00.
Joaquin Oil & Mining Co., San Francisco, capital, $10,000; uar value,, $1.00.
Juanita Oil Co., Los Angeles, capital, $10,000,000; par value, $1.00.

Jacalitas Petroleum Co., San Francisco, capital, $250,000; par value, $5.00.
Jewett-Blodgett-Beal Oil Co., Bakersfield, capital, $500,000; par value, $1.00.
J. S. Potts Oil Land & Development Co., San Francisco, capital, $600,000; par value, $1.00.
John Thomas Oil Co., Los Angeles, capital, $336,000; par value, $1.00.
Jennings Oil Co., San Francisco, capital $90,000; par value, $100.00.
Juanita Oil Mining & Development Co., Oakland, capital, $150.000; par value, $1.00.
Juniper Oil Co., Los Angeles, capital, $500,000; par value, $1.00.
Junction Oil Co., Bakersfield, capital, $250,000; par value, $1.00.
Jewett Oil Co., Bakersfield, capital, $500,000; par value, $1.00.
Kreyenhagen Land & Oil Co., Los Angeles, capital, $100,000; par value, $100.00.
Kern Canyon Oil Co., Hanford, capital, $100,000; par value, $25.00.
Keystone Oil Co., Fresno, capital, $100,000; par value, $10.00.
Keystone Oil & Development Co., Dinuba, capital, $150,000; par value, $1.00.
Kern Canyon Oil Co., Fresno, capital, $200,000; par value, $2.00.
Kings County Oil Co., San Francisco, capital, $100,000; par value, $1.00.
Kismet Oil Co., Los Angeles, capital, $500,000; par value, $1.00.
Keystone Refining Co., San Francisco, capital, $150,000; par value, $100.00.
Keystone Oil & Development Co., Los Angeles, capital, $500,000; par value, $1.00.
King Solomon Oil & Mining Co., San Francisco, capital, $100,000; par value, $1.00.
King Oil Co., San Francisco, capital, $250,000; par value, $1.00.
Kettleman Hill Petroleum Co., Oakland, capital, $200,000; par value, $1.00.
Kettleman Oil & Gas Co., Lemoore, capital $200,000; par value, $1.00.
Kern Oil Co., Bakersfield, capital, $100,000; par value, $1.00.
Kern Delta Oil Co., Oakland, capital, $500,000; par value, $1.00.
Kern River Oil & Development Co., San Francisco, capital, $250,000; par value, $1.00.
Keystone Oil Co., Los Angeles, capital, $150,000; par value $5.00.
Kern Central Oil Co., Los Angeles, capital, $100,000; par value $1.00.
Kern County Oil Co., San Francisco, capital, $200,000; par value, $2.00;
Kern Consolidated Oil Co., Los Angeles, capital, $300,000; par value $1.00.
King Keystone Oil Co., San Francisco, capital, $50,000; par value, $100.00.
King Bee Oil Co., Bakersfield, capital, $100,000; par value, $1.00.
Kings Co. Oil Development Co., San Francisco, capital, $200,000; par value, $1.00.
Knob Hill Oil Co., Fresno, $25,000; par value, $5000.00.
K. T. Oil Co., Los Angeles, capital, $250,000; par value, $1.00.
Lake View Land & Oil Co., Hanford, capital, $200,000; par value $1.00.
Lakeside Land & Oil Development Co., Hanford, capital, $300,000; par value, $1.00.
Las Lucecitas Oil & Development Co., San Francisco, capital, $200,000; par value $1.00.
Lewis Creek Oil Co., Hollister, capital, $100,000; par value, $10.00.
Le Roi Oil Co., San Francisco, $100,000; par value, $1.00.
Lincoln Oil Co., Lincoln, capital, $500,000; par value, $5.00.
Little San Oil Co., San Francisco, capital, 250,000; par value, $5.00.
Loma Vista Petroleum Co., Los Angeles, capital, $100,000; par value, $1.00.
London Oil Co., Selma, capital, $500,000; par value, $5.00.
London Oil Co., San Francisco, capital, $700,000; par value, $1.00.
Lone Star Oil Co., Bakersfield, capital, $500,000; par value, $1.00.
Los Angeles Oil & Transfer Co., San Francisco, capital, $250,000; par value, $25.00.
Leaming Petroleum Co., San Francisco, capital, $1,000,000; par value, $100.00.
Lincoln Petroleum Mining Co., Eureka, capital, $128,000; par value, $100.00.
Liverpool Petroleum Co., San Francisco, capital, $6,000,000; par value, $100.00.
Livermore Oil Co., San Francisco, capital, $1,000,000; par value, $10.00.
Lagomarsino Oil Co., Los Angeles, capital, $500,000; par value, $1.00.
Little Joker Oil Co., Los Angeles, capital, $250,000; par value, $1.00.
La Fiesta Oil Co., San Francisco, $250,000; par value, $5.00.
Los Banos Oil Co., San Francisco, capital, $200,000; par value, $1.00.
Laguna Oil Co., Santa Ana, capital, $600,000; par value, $1.00.
Lookout Mountain Oil Co., Pasadena, capital, $1,000,000; par value, $1.00.
Lion Oil Co., Los Angeles, capital, $100,000; par value, $1.00.
Lincoln Oil Co., Los Angeles, capital, $400,000; par value, $1.00.
Los Angeles Oil & Investment Co., Los Angeles, capital, $100,000; par value, $1.00.
Lithograph Canyon Oil & Mining Co., Randsburg, capital, $100,000; par value $1.00.
Lighthouse Oil Co., Los Angeles, capital, $300,000; par value, $1.00.
Lucky Nine Oil Co., Bakersfield, capital, $600,000; par value, $1.00.
La Jolla Oil Co., San Diego, capital, $500,000; par value, $1.00.
Leased Land Oil Co., San Francisco, capital, $5,000,000; par value, $1000.00.
Live Oak Oil Co., Los Angeles, capital; $600,000; par value, $1.00.
Lexington Oil Co., Los Angeles, capital, $600,000; par value, $1.00.
Lopez Canyon Oil Co., Los Angeles, capital, $200,000; par value, $1.00.
Liberty Oil Co., Los Angeles, capital, $300,000; par value, $1.00.
Lord Roberts Oil Co., Hanford, capital, $20,000; par value, $250.00.
Lemoore Oil Co., Lemoore, capital, $300,000 par value, $10.00.
Little Tar Canyon Oil Co., Hanford, capital, $100,000; par value, $1.00.
Lion Oil & Asphalt Co., Ventura, capital, $200,000; par value, $100.00.
Louisa Petroleum Co., San Francisco, capital, $500,000; par value, $10.00
La Verdad Oil Co., Los Angeles, capital, $500,000; par value, $1.00.
Lencadia Oil Co., Oakland capital, $250,000; par value, $1.00.
La Corona Oil & Asphalt Co., Bakersfield, capital, $190,000; par value, $10.00.
Livermore Natural Oil & Gas Co., Livermore, capital, $20,000; par value, $10.00.
Little Cholame Oil & Mining Co., Bakersfield, capital, $7,000; par value, $10.00.
Loma Oil Co., Los Angeles, capital, $50,000; par value, $100.00,
Los Angeles Oil Co., Los Angeles, capital, $50,000; par value, $10.00.
Los Angeles Petroleum Smelting and Mining Co., Los Angeles, capital, $200,000; par value, $10.00.
Leavitt-Lassen Oil Co., Susanville, capital, $300,000; par value, $1.00.
Mallory Oil Co., Stockton, capital, $100,000; par value, $1.00.
Mammoth Oil Co., Fresno, capital, $300,000; par value, $1.00.
Marguerite Oil & Mining Co., Visalia, capital, $50,000; par value, $50.00.
Marietta Oil Co., Oakland, capital. $5,000; par value, $5.00.
Matthews Oil Co., Selma, capital, $200,000; par value, $1.00.
McKittrick Petroleum & Development Co., San Francisco, capital, $1,000,000; par value, $1.00.

McCray Bros. Crude Oil Co., Los Angeles, capital, $500,000; par value, $1.00.
McKittrick Consolidated Oil Co., San Francisco, capital, $600,000; par value, $10,00.
McCoy Oil Co., Hanford, capital, $250,000; par value, $1.00.
McCray, Bros. Oil Co., Los Angeles, capital, $100,000; par value, $100.00.
Mendota Oil Co., San Francisco, capital, $500,-000; par value, $5,00.
Mendota Oil & Development Co., San Francisco, capital, $100,000; par value, $1.00.
Melrose Land & Oil Co., San Francisco, capital, $50,000; par value, $1.00.
Mercy Oil Co., Fresno, capital, $200,000; par value, $1.00.
Merchants Mutual Oil Co., San Francisco, capital, $200,000; par value, $5.00.
Merchants' Oil Co., San Francisco, capital, $50,000; par value, $1.00.
Merced Oil Mining Co., Merced, capital, $1,000,-000; par value, $1.00.
Midway Oil Co., Bakersfield, capital, $10,-par value, $1.00.
Midon Oil & Development Co., San Francisco, capital, $500,000; par value, $5.00.
Missouri Oil Co., Fresno, capital, $160,000; par value, $10.00.
Modesto Oil Co., Modesto, capital, $200,000; par value, $1.00.
Monterey Oil Corporation, Los Angeles, capital, $500,000; par value, $1.00.
Montana Oil Co., Oakland, capital, $200,000; par value, 10.00.
Monterey Oil Co., Monterey, capital, $1,000,000; par value, $1.00.
Montjac Oil Mining Co., San Francisco, capital, $100,000; par value, $1.00.
Monte Cristo Oil & Development Co., San Francisco, capital, $500,000; par value, $1.00.
Montezuma Oil Co., San Francisco, capital, $1,000,000; par value $5.00.
Monarch Oil Co., San Diego, capital, $1,000,-000; par value, $1.00.
Morris Jones Oil Co., Los Angeles, capital, $4,000; par value, $10.00.
Morningside Oil Co., Los Angeles capital, $500,-000; par value, $100.00.
Mt. Diablo Oil Co., San Francisco, capital, $500,000; par value, $1.00.
Mt. Adelaide Oil & Mining Co., Kern, capital, $250,000; par value, $1.00.
Mt. Vernon Oil Co., Oakland capital, $500,000; par value, $1.00.
Mt. Diablo Oil Mining & Development Co., Fresno, capital, $500,000; par value, $1.00.
Mutual Mineral Oil Co., San Francisco, capital, $100,000; par value $1.00.
Mustavit Oil Co., Visalia, capital, $225,000; par value, $5.00.
Minerva Oil Co., Los Angeles, capital, $50,-000; par value, $1.00.
Mojave Oil & Pipe Line Co., Los Angeles, capital, $500,000; par value, $1.00.
Miocene Oil Co., Stockton, capital, $75,000; par value, $5.00.
Mutual Oil Co., Selma, capital, $250,000; par value, $100.00.
Mt. Goddard Oil Co., Fresno, capital, $200,000; par value, $1.00.
Million Oil Co., Fresno, capital, $1000.00; par value, $1.00.
Martinez Oil Co., Fresno, capital, $50,000; par value, $10.00.
Moody Gulch Oil Co., Los Angeles, capital, $150,000; par value, $100.00.
Monarch Oil Co., Bakersfield, capital, $100,-000; par value, $1.00.
Monarch Oil Co., San Francisco, capital, $500,-000; par value, $5.00.
Magic Oil Co., San Francisco, capital, $600,000; par value, $1.00.
Marine Oil Co. of Summerland & Los Angeles, Los Angeles, capital, $300,000; par value, $1.00.
Midland Oil Co., Los Angeles, capital, $350,000; par value, $1.00.
Morse Oil Co., Santa Ana, capital, $100,000; par value, $1.00.
Maltese Cross Oil Co., Los Angeles, capital, $200,000; par value, $1.00.
McWhorter Oil Refining Co., Kern, capital, $100,000; par value, $1.00.
Mercantile Oil Co., Los Angeles, $250,000; par value, $1.00.
Morning Star Oil & Mining Co., Los Angeles, capital, $600,000; par value, $1.00.
Menges Oil Co., Santa Ana, capital, $90,000; par value, $1.00.
Mohawk Oil Co., Bakersfield, capital, $250,000; par value, $1.00.
Morris Jones Oil & Fuel Co., Los Angeles, capital, $100,000; par value, $1.00.
Mt. Shasta Oil & Development Co., San Francisco, capital, $250,000; par value, $1.00
Mansfield Oil & Water Co., Los Angeles, capital, $250,000; par value, $1.00.
Mesquite Oil Co., Los Angeles, capital, $400,-000; par value, $1.00.
Mother Lode Oil Co., Hanford, capital, $200,-000; par value, $1.00.
Morning Star Oil Co., Selma, capital, $50,000; par value, $25.00.
Maximus Oil & Development Co., Fresno, capital, $500,000; par value, $10.00.
McKittrick Central Oil Co., San Francisco, capital, $100,000; par value, $1.00.
Monitor Oil Co., San Francisco, capital, $100,-000; par value, $1.00.
Madera Oil Co., Madera, capital, $100,000; par value, $1.00.
Mutual Benefit Oil Co., Los Angeles, capital, $100,000; par value, $1.00.
McFayden Oil Co., San Francisco, capital, $200,000; par value, $1.00.
Madera Crude Oil Co., Madera, capital, $100,-000; par value, $1.00.
Murrietta Oil & Development Co., Los Angeles, capital, $200,000; par value, $1.00.
Metropolitan Oil Co., Los Angeles, capital, $100,000; par value, $1.00.
Mutual Oil Co., Whittier, capital, $50,000; par value, $1.00.
Modelo Oil Co., San Francisco, capital, $250,000; par value, $100.00.
Mattole Creek Oil Co., San Francisco, capital, $200,000; par value, $100.00.
Mattole Petroleum Co., San Francisco, capital, $200,000; par value, $100.00.
McCullough & Preston Petroleum Co., San Francisco, $500,000; par value, $10.00.
Merchants Petroleum Co., San Francisco, capital, $800,000; par value, $100.00.
Mexican Oil & Gas Co., Los Angeles, capital, $2,000,000; par value, $20.00.
Monarch Oil & Gas Co., Los Angeles, capital, $250,000; par value, $10.00.
Mountain View Petroleum Mining Co., Los Angeles, capital, $200,000; par value, $10,000.
Mupu Oil Co., San Francisco, capital, $500,000; par value, $10.00.
Mutual Oil Co., San Francisco capital, $100,000; par value, $100.00.
Mission Mines Oil Co., San Francisco, capital, $500,000; par value, $1.00.
National Oil Co., Stockton, capital, $500,000; par value, $5.00.
National Oil Development Co., Sacramento, capital, $75,000; par value, $10.00.
National Oil Co., Oakland, capital, $100,000; par value, $1.00.
New Standard Oil Co., San Francisco, capital, $150,000; par value, $2.50.
New Hope Oil Co., San Francisco, capital, $100,000; par value, $1.00.
New Dominion Oil Co., Los Angeles, capital, $100,000; par value, $1.00.
Newhall Oil & Development Co., San Francisco, capital, $500,000; par value, $1.00.
New Century Oil Co., Los Angeles, capital, $1,000,000; par value, $1.00.
New Mexico Oil Development Co., Los Angeles, capital, $250,000; par value, $1.00.
Ninty-nine Oil Co., Oakland, capital, $100,000; par value, $1.00.
Nonpareil Petroleum Co., San Francisco, capital, $100,000; par value, $5.00.

Northfield Oil Co., Fresno, capital, $200,000; par value, $1.00.
North Star Drilling & Oil Co., Bakersfield, capital, $250,000; par value, $2.50.
Nueva Coal & Oil Co., Los Angeles, capital, $50,000; par value, $10.00.
Nueva Camulos Oil Co., Los Angeles, capital, $200,000; par value, $1.00.
North Whittier Oil Co., Los Angeles, capital, $200,000; par value, $1.00.
Natural Oil Co., San Francisco, capital, $200,000; par value, $1.00.
Natural Gas & Oil Co., Los Angeles, capital, $1,000,000; par value, $10.00.
National Oil Co., Los Angeles, capital, $2500.00; par value, $10.00.
Napa Oil Co., San Francisco, capital, $250,000; par value, $100.00.
New York Oil Co., Fresno, capital, $100,000; par value, $100.00.
Northern California Oil Co., Red Bluff, capital, $200,000; par value, $1.00.
Nettleton & Kellerman Oil Co., Los Angeles, capital, $600,000; par value, $1.00.
Northern Oil Co., Santa Paula, capital, $150,000; par value, $3.00.
Northern Consolidated Oil & Mining Co., Los Angeles, capital, $5,000,000; par value, $1.00.
National, Oil & Mining Co., Los Angeles, capital, $1,000,000; par value, $1.00.
Northern Consolidated Oil & Mining Co., Los Angeles, capital, $1,000,000; par value, $1.00.
New San Pedro Oil Co., San Pedro, capital, $500,000; par value, $1.00.
New Baltimore Oil Co., Bakersfield, capital, $15,000; par value, $1.00.
New Era Oil & Water Co., Los Angeles, capital, $500,000; par value, $1.00.
Niagara Oil Co., San Francisco, capital, $100,000; par value, $1.00.
New England Oil Co., Los Angeles, capital, $300,000; par value, $10.00.
Napa Petroleum Co., Napa, capital, $600,000; par value, $100.00.
Naphtha Oil Spring Co., San Joaquin, capital, $700,000; par value, $20.00.
National Oil Co., San Francisco, capital, $150,000; par value, $100.00.
Newhall Oil & Pipe Line Co., Los Angeles, capital, $12,000; par value, $100.00.
Newhall & Castaic Oil Mining Co., capital, $400,000; par value, $1.00.
North Buena Vista Oil Co., San Francisco, capital, $500,000; par value, $10.00.
Nueva Puente Oil Co., Los Angeles, capital, $250,000; par value, $100.00.
Newport Oil Co., Santa Ana, capital, $50,000; par value, $10.00.
Nob Hill Oil & Development Co., Los Angeles, capital, $150,000; par value, $25.00.
Orange Center Oil Co., Lindsey, capital, $200,000; par value, $5.00.
Oil Center Co., Bakersfield, capital, $250,000; par value, $1.00.
Oil Fuel Saving Co., San Francisco, capital, $150,000; par value, $1.00.
Our Own Company, McKittrick, capital, $100,000; par value, $1000.00.
Occidental Oil Mining & Development Co., San Francisco, capital, $1,000,000; par value, $1.00.
Oil Spring Oil Co., Oakland, capital, $250,000; par value, $1.00.
Ocean View Oil Co., Los Angeles, capital, $200,000; par value, $1.00.
Old Glory Oil Co., Bakersfield, capital, $300,000; par value, $1.00.
Ocean Front Oil Co., Los Angeles, capital, $100,000; par value, $1.00.
Operators Oil Co., Bakersfield, capital, $100,000; par value, $100.00.
Ohio Oil Co. of San Francisco, San Francisco, capital, $300,000; par value, $1.00.
Ocean View Oil & Development Co., Pomona, capital, $300,000; par value, $1.00.
Oscar Bonner Oil Co., Los Angeles, capital, $150,000; par value, $1.00.
Oxnard Oil Co., Oxnard, capital, $500,000; par value, $1.00.
Ojai Valley Oil Co., Los Angeles, capital, $600,000; par value, $1.00.
Oil, Asphalt & Water Co. of Southern California, Los Angeles, capital, $1,000,000; par value, $100.00.
Oil Lake Fuel Co., Los Angeles, capital, $300,000, par value, $1.00.
Owl Oil Co., San Francisco, capital, $100,000; par value, $1.00.
Owl Oil Co., San Francisco, capital, $500,000; par value, $5.00.
Occident Oil Co., San Francisco, capital, $600,000; par value, $10.00.
Occidental Mining Oil & Development Co., San Francisco, $1,000,000; par value, $1.00.
Oil Center Petroleum Co., Fresno, capital, $250,000; par value, $1.00.
Ophir Oil & Development Co., Fresno, capital, $500,000; par value, $1.00.
Ocean Coast Oil Co., Los Angeles, capital, $500,000; par value, $100.00.
Ocean View Oil Co., Los Angeles, capital, $200,000; par value, $1.00.
Oil Canyon Co., Los Angeles, capital, $500,000; par value, $1.00.
Ojai Oil Co., Los Angeles, capital, $750,000; par value, $1.00.
Occidental Petroleum Co., Princeton, capital, $625,000; par value, $25.00.
Occidental Oil Refining Co., Los Angeles, capital, $250,000; par value, $5.00.
Occidental Mining & Petroleum Co., Santa, Barbara, capital, $500,000; par value, $10.00.
Oil Creek Petroleum Co., Eureka, capital, $50,000; par value, $500.00.
Oil Hill Petroleum Co., Oakland, capital, $600,000; par value, $10.00.
Oak Oil Co., Los Angeles, capital, $500,000; par value, $1.00.
Oakland Oil Co., Oakland, capital, $20,000; par value, $5.00.
Oceanic Oil & Fuel Co., Hanford, $200,000; par value, $1.00.
Oceanic Oil Co., Los Angeles, capital, $150,000; par value, $1.00.
Occidental Oil & Development Co. of California, Stockton, capital, $200,000; par value, $1.00.
O'Donnell Oil Co., Los Angeles, capital, $250,000; par value, $100.00.
Oil Queen Co., San Francisco, capital, $100,000; par value, $1.00.
Oil King Co., San Francisco, capital, $100,000; par value, $1.00.
Oil Producers' Association, San Francisco, capital, $100,000; par value, $1.00.
Oil Spring Petroleum Co., Fresno, $100,000; par value, $1.00.
Old Dominion Oil Co., San Jose, capital, $100,000; par value, $5.00.
Olympia Oil Land & Development Co., Sacramento, capital, $200,000; par value, $1.00.
Omega Oil & Development Co., Oakland, capital, $500,000; par value, $1.00.
Oriental Oil & Development Co., San Francisco, capital, $100,000; par value, $1.00.
Oriental Oil Co., San Francisco, capital, $100,000; par value, $1.00.
Orange Oil Co., Santa Ana, capital, $50,000; par value, $1.00.
Oakland Oil & Asphalt Co., Oakland, capital, $64,000; par value, $1.00.
Occident Oil Co., Fresno, capital, $32,000; par value, $25.00.
Oil City Petroleum Co., Fresno, $500,000; par value, $100.00.
Olally Oil Co., Selma, capital, $50,000; par value, $100.00.
Oregon Oil Co., Hanford, capital, $68,000; par value, $100.00;
Oxnard Oil Co., Santa Barbara, capital, $100,000; par value, $1.00.
Palo Solo Oil Co., Los Angeles, capital, $100,000; par value, $1.00.
Pacific Oil Mining & Development Co., San Francisco, capital, $500,000; par value, $1.00.
Park Crude Oil Co., Los Angeles, capital, $100,000; par value, $1.00.
Pasadena Oil Co., Pasadena, capital, $100,000; par value, $1.00.

Pennsylvania Oil Co. of San Francisco, San Francisco, capital, $100,000; par value, $1.00.
Pennsylvania Consolidated Oil Co., San Francisco, capital, $500,000; par value, $5.00.
Peerless Oil Co., San Francisco, capital, $1,000,000; par value, $10.00.
Pennsylvania Oil Co. of California, Oakland, capital, $100,000; par value, $1.00.
Petrolia Land & Oil Co., Oakland, capital, $6400.00; par value, $1.00.
Petroleum Center Oil Co., San Francisco, capital, $500,000; par value, $1.00.
Pierpont Oil Co., San Francisco, capital, $100,000; par value, $1.00.
Pioneer Oil & Gas Co. of Kern County, Hanford, capital, $400,000; par value, $1000.00.
Pittsburg Oil Co., Bakersfield, capital, $300,000; par value, $1.00.
Pliocene Oil Co., San Francisco, capital, $100,000; par value, $1.00.
Point Arena Oil & Land Co., Point Arena, capital, $750,000; par value, $5.00.
Polvedero Oil Mining Co., Visalia, capital, $50,000; par value, $100.00.
Pony Capital Oil Co., Sanger, capital, $135,000; par value, $10.00.
Poso Oil Co., Bakersfield, capital, $100,000; par value, $1.00.
Poston Oil Co., San Jose, capital, $300,000; par value, $10.00.
President Oil Co., Bakersfield, capital, $400,000; par value, $1.00.
Providence Crude Oil Co., San Francisco, capital, $500,000; par value, $10.00.
Plymouth Rock Oil Co., Oakland, capital, $500,000; par value, $1.00.
Pennsylvania Oil Co., Los Angeles, capital, $250,000; par value, $1.00.
Pacific Slope Oil & Development Co., Bakersfield, capital, $200,000; par value, $1.00.
Porterville, Oil & Mining Co., Porterville, capital, $100,000; par value, $1.00.
Padua Oil Co., Los Angeles, capital, $300,000; par value, $1.00.
Palace Oil Co., San Francisco, capital, $1,000,000; par value, $1.00.
Parker Oil. Co., Los Angeles, capital, $250,000; par value, $1.00.
Petrolia Oil Co., Tulare, capital, $50,000; par value, $10.00.
Pacific Petroleum Co., Selma, capital, $800,000; par value, $100.00.
Parkfield Oil Co., Fresno, capital, $200,000; par value, $100.00.
Petroleum Development Co., Los Angeles, capital, $125,000; par value, $1.00.
Phoenix Oil Co., Hanford, capital, $100,000; par value, $100.00.
Pittsburg Oil Co., Oakland, capital, $300,000; par value, $1.00.
Pacific Slope Oil Co., Los Angeles, capital, $500,000; par value, $1.00.
Paso Robles Oil & Development, Co., Paso Robles, capital, $150,000; par value, $1.00.
Pico Oil Co. of Los Angeles, Los Angeles, capital, $300,000; par value, $1.00.
Pioneer White Oil Co., Los Angeles, capital, $300,000; par value, $1.00.
Placerita White Oil Co., Los Angeles, capital, $1,500,000; par value, $1.00.
Progressive Woman's Oil Co., San Francisco, capital, $100,000; par value, $1.00.
Piru Consolidated Oil Co., Los Angeles, capital, $352,000; par value, $10.00.
Plato Oil & Development Co., Selma, capital, $400,000; par value, $1.00.
Pacific Coast Petroleum Co., San Francisco, capital, $50,000; par value, $10.00.
Pacific Coast Oil Co., San Francisco, capital, $1,000,000; par value, $10.00.
Pacific Coast Oil Co., San Francisco, capital, $1,000,000; par value, $10.00.
Pacific Consolidated Petroleum Mining Co., Redding, capital, $100,000; par value, $1.00.
Pacific Coast Natural Gas, Oil & Mineral Co., San Francisco, capital, $100,000; par value, $10.00.
Pacific Oil Co., Eureka, capital, $500,000; par value, $10.00.
Pacific Oil & Land Co., San Francisco, capital, $10,000,000; par value, $100.00.
Partfield Oil Co., San Miguel, capital, $150,000; par value, $100.00.
Paragon Oil Co., Los Angeles, capital, $400,000, par value, $20.00.
Pennsylvania Petroleum Co., San Francisco, capital, $300,000; par value, $100.00.
Pennsylvania Petroleum Oil Co., Santa Cruz, capital, $100,000; par value, $100.00.
Petrolia Asphaltum & Oil Co., San Francisco, capital, $350,000; par value, $10.00.
Petrolia Oil & Transportation Co., San Francisco, capital, $500,000; par value, $5.00.
Phoenix Petroleum Co., San Francisco, capital, $5,000,000; par value, $100.00.
Piru Oil Co., Los Angeles, capital, $100,000; par value, $100.00.
Puente Oil Co., Los Angeles, capital, $1,000,000; par value, $100.00.
Pioneer Petroleum Refining Co., San Francisco, capital, $50,000; par value, $1000.00.
Pioneer Petroleum Mining Co., San Francisco, capital, $120,000; par value, $50.00.
Primrose Crude Oil Co., Los Angeles, capital, $500,000; par value, $1.00.
Prudential Oil & Development Co., San Francisco, capital, $100,000; par value, $1.00.
Pure Oil Co. of Santa Paula, Los Angeles, capital, $300,000; par value, $1.00.
Palomas Oil Co., Los Angeles, capital, $1,000,000; par value, $1.00.
Puritan Oil Mining Co., Long Beach, capital, $600,000; par value, $20.00.
Pitcher & Garbutt Oil Co., Los Angeles, capital, $500,000; par value, $1.00.
Pacific Union Oil Co., Los Angeles, capital, $500,000; par value, $1.00.
Pine Oil & Land Co., Los Angeles, capital, $3,000,000; par value, $1.00.
Point Richmond Oil Co., San Francisco, capital, $100,000; par value, $1.00.
Prudential Mining & Oil Development Co., Los Angeles, capital, $750,000; par value, $1.00.
Petroleum Development Co. of California, San Francisco, capital, $500,000; par value, $1.00.
Panoche Oil & Mineral Co., Fresno, capital, $200,000; par value, $1.00.
Postal Union Oil Mining & Development, Co., Los Angeles, capital, $500,000; par value, $1.00.
Phelps Petroleum Co., San Francisco, capital, $500,000; par value, $1.00.
Panoche Coast Range Oil Co., Merced, capital, $200,000; par value. $1.00.
Pleasant Valley Oil Co., Los Angeles, capita, $25,000; par value, $1.00.
Pleasant Valley Oil Co., Fresno, capital, $500,000; par value, $100.00.
Phoenix Oil Co., Los Angeles, capital, $40,000; par value, $100.00.
Petroleum & Coal Development Co. of Guatemala, San Francisco, $1,400,000; par value, $100.00.
Producers' & Consumers' Oil Co., Fresno, capital, $1,000,000; par value, $100.00.
Petrolia Paraffine Oil Co., San Francisco, capital, $100,000; par value, $1.00.
Pacific Oil Production Co., Los Angeles, capital, $320,000; par value, $10,00.
Pacoima Oil Co., Los Angeles, capital, $150,000; par value, $1.00.
Pacific Mutual Oil Co., Oakland, capital, $100,000; par value, $1.00.
Pearl Oil Co., Los Angeles, capital, $300,000; par value, $10.00.
Paidup Oil Co., Los Angeles, capital, $2,000; par value, $50.00.
Port Harford Oil Co., San Francisco, capital, $200,000; par value, $1.00.
Prudential Mining & Oil Development Co., Los Angeles, capital, $750,000; par value, $1.00.
Puente Hill Oil Co., Los Angeles, capital, $350,000; par value, $1.00.
Quito Oil Mining & Development Co., Oakland, capital, $100,000; par value, $1.00.
Queen Oil Co., Los Angeles, capital, $250,000; par value, $1.00.
Redding Oil & Imporvement Co., Redding, capital, $100,000; par value, $1.00.

Rodeo Oil Co. of Los Angeles, Los Angeles, capital, $100,000; par value, $1.00.
Rival Oil Co., Los Angeles, capital, $300,000; par value, $1.00.
Raymond Oil Co., Pasadena, capital, $500,000; par value, $1.00.
Rancho La Presa Oil & Mining Co., San Diego, capital, $5,000,000; par value, $1.00.
Rincon Petroleum Co., Los Angeles & Redlands, capital, $500,000; par value, $1.00.
Redondo Beach Oil Co., Los Angeles, capital, $300,000; par value, $1.00.
R. G. R. Petroleum & Mining Co., Santa Barbara, capital, $100,000; par value, $1.00.
Rotary Oil Drilling Co., Los Angeles, capital, $500,000; par value, $1.00.
Royal Union Oil Co., Los Angeles, capital, $600,000; par value, $1.00.
Reliance Oil Co., Los Angeles, capital, $125,000; par value, $1.00.
Rowland Puente Oil Co., Covina, capital, $500,000; par value, $1.00.
Red Cross Oil Co., Los Angeles, capital $250,000; par value $1.00.
Reed Crude Oil Co., Los Angeles, capital $2,000,000; par value, $1.00.
Raymond Oil Co., Los Angeles, capital, $50,000; par value $1.00.
Rex Oil Co., Los Angeles, capital, $50,000; par value $100.00.
Rainbow Oil Co., Santa Paula, capital $50,000; par value $100.00.
Rowland & Lacy Petroleum and Land Co., Los Angeles, capital, $1,000,000; par value, $100.00.
Royal Oil Co. of Coalinga, Fresno, capital, $500,000; par value, $50.00.
Railway Men's Oil Co., Los Angeles, capital, $300,000; par value, $1.00.
Ramona Oil Co. of Los Angeles & Ventura Co., Los Angeles, capital, $300,000; par value, $1.00.
Raven Pass Oil Co., Los Angeles, capital, $300,000; par value, $1.00.
Red Rock Oil & Mining Co., Pasadena, capital, $250,000; par value, $1.00.
Reed Oil Co., Los Angeles, capital, $1,000,000; par value, $10.00.
Reedley Oil Co., Reedley, $250,000; par value, $10.00.
Rex Crude, Oil Co., San Francisco, capital, $300,000; par value, $5.00.
Revenue Oil Co., Pasadena, capital, $200,000; par value, $1.00.
Rice Canyon Oil Co., Los Angeles, capital, $200,000; par value, $100.00.
Richmond Oil & Fuel Co., San Francisco, capital, $250,000; par value, $1.00.
Rising Sun Oil & Development Co., Bakersfield, capital, $250,000; par value, $1.00.
Rio Bravo Oil Co., San Francisco, capital, $100,000; par value, $1.00.
River View Oil Co., Santa Cruz, capital, $50,000; par value, $2.00.
Rodeo Valley. Oil Co., Fresno, capital, $1,000,000; par value, $1.00.
Rommel Oil Co., Los Angeles, capital, $500,000; par value, $1.00.
Royal Eagle Oil Co., Bakersfield, capital, 250,000; par value, $1.00.
Riverside Crude Oil Co., Los Angeles, capital, $500,000; par value, $1.00.
Sacramento Oil Co., Sacramento, capital, $100,000; par value, $1.00.
Sand Hill Crude Oil Co., Hanford, capital, $200,000; par value, $100.00.
San Ardo Petroleum Co., San Francsco, capital, $60,000; par value, $5.00.
San Antonio Oil & Land Co., San Francisco, capital, $100,000; par value, $1.00.
San Fernando Oil Co., San Francisco, capital, $500,000; par value, $1.00.
Sanger & Fresno Oil Co., capital, $250,000; par value, $10.00.
Sanger Oil & Gas Co., Sanger, capital, $100,000; par value, $1.00.
San Joaquin Oil Co., Hanford, capital,, $50,000; par value, $10.00.
San Juan Oil Co., San Francisco, capital, $500,000; par value, $1.00.
San Joaquin Oil & Development Co., Fresno, capital, $100,000; par value, $1.00.
San Jose Petroleum Co. of Panoche, San Jose, capital, $500,000; par value, $1.00.
San Luis Oil Co., San Francisco, capital, $1,000,000; par value, $10.00.
San Pablo Oil Co., San Francisco, capital, $100,000; par value, $1.00.
Santa Clara Oil Co. of Coalinga, San Jose, capital, $500,000; par value, $50.00.
Santa Fe Oil Co., Los Angeles, capital, $1,000,000; par value, $10.00.
Santa Susana Oil Co., Los Angeles, capital, $500,000; par value, $5.00.
Selby Oil & Mining Co., Los Angeles, capital, $150,000; par value, $1.00.
Sequoia Oil Mining Co., Fresno, capital, $200,000; par value, $1.00.
Sequoia Oil & Development Co., Visalia, capital, $250,000; par value, $2.50.
Sespe Oil Co., Los Angeles, capital, $250,000; par value, $1.00.
Shamrock Oil Co., San Francsico, capital, $250,000; par value, $2,50.
Shafter Oil & Development Co., Bakersfield, capital $100,000; par value, $1.00.
Shale Basin Oil Co., Selma, capital, $100,000; par value, $1.00.
Sierra Oil & Fuel Co. of California, San Francisco, capital, $200,000; par value, $20.00.
Sobrante Oil & Investment Co., San Francisco, capital, $500,000; par value, $1.00.
Southern Pacific Oil & Improvement Co., San Francisco, capital, $500,000; par value, $5.00.
Southern California Oil & Fuel Co., Los Angeles, capital, $300,000; par value, $1.00.
Southern Consolidated Oil Co., Los Angeles, capital, $300,000; par value, $1.00.
St. Bernard Oil Co., Los Angeles, capital, $200,000; par value, $1.00.
St. John Oil Co., Visalia, capital, $100,000; par value, $2.00.
Stella Oil Mining Co., San Francisco, capital, $100,000; par value, $1.00.
Seacoast Land & Oil Co., Los Angeles, capital, $500,000; par value, $1.00.
Southern Pacific Gold & Oil Developement Co., San Francisco, capital, $1,000,000; par value, $1.00.
Senator Oil Co., Bakersfield, capital, $200,000; par value, $1.00.
Simi Oil Co., Los Angeles, capital, $600,000; par value, $1.00.
State Mutual Oil Co., Los Angeles, capital, $1,000,000; par value, $1.00.
Sierra Oil Co., Los Angeles, capital, $250,000; par value, $1.00.
Santa Paula Oil Co., Los Angeles, capital, $300,000; par value, $1.00.
Sulphur Mountain Oil Co., Santa Ana, capital, $500,000; par value, $1.00.
Summerland Oil Storage Co. of Summerland & Los Angeles, Los Angeles, capital, $50,000; par value, $1.00.
Sunset District Oil Co., San Francisco, capital, $300,000; par value, $1.00.
Santa Barbara Oil & Development Co., Bakersfield, capital, $500,000; par value, $1.00.
Santiago Oil & Development Co., Santa Ana, capital, $200,000; par value, $1.00.
Summerland Oil & Land Co., San Francisco, capital, $250,000; par value, $1.00.
South Coast Oil & Mining Co., Los Angeles, capital, $400,000; par value, $1.00.
Summit Oil Co., San Francisco, capital, $100,000; par value, $1.00.
Santa Barbara & Kern Co. Oil Co., Santa Barbara, capital, $150,000; par value, $1.00.
Sunset Queen Oil Co., Los Angeles, capital, $300,000; par value, $1.00.
Sherman Oil Co., Los Angeles, capital, $400,000; par value, $1.00.
Sunshine Oil Co., Los Angeles, capital, $250,000; par value, $1.00.
Sheridan Oil Co., Los Angeles, capital, $500,000; par value, $1.00.
South-Coast Oil Co., Los Angeles, capital, $300,000; par value, $1.00.

San Pedro Oil Co., San Pedro, capital, $500,000; par value, $1.00.
Singer Oil Co., San Francisco, capital, $500,000; par value, $5.00.
Southern Counties Oil Co., Los Angeles, capital, $300,000; par value, $1.00.
Seneca Oil Co., Los Angeles, capital, $500,000; par value, $1.00.
Safe Oil Co., Los Angeles, capital, $500,000; par value, $1.00.
Sultan Oil Co., Los Angeles, capital, $500,000; par value, $1.00.
Sea Breeze Oil Co., Bakersfield, capital, $500,000; par value, $1.00.
Swiss-American Oil & Development Co., San Francisco, capital, $200,000; par value, $1.00.
Simi Crude Oil Co., Los Angeles, capital, $750,000; par value, $1.00.
Southern Cross Drill & Oil Co., Bakersfield, capital, $250,000; par value, $1.00.
Santa Ana Crude Oil Co., Santa Ana, capital, $500,000; par value, $1.00.
Sunset Coast Oil Co., Los Angeles, capital, $500,000; par value, $1.00.
Sacramento Oil Development Co., Sacramento, capital, $32,000; par value, $1.00.
Sunset Consolidated Oil Co., Los Angeles, capital, $750,000; par value, $1.00.
Sulphur Mountain Petroleum Co., Fullerton, capital, $800,000; par value, $1.00.
Santa Ana & Bakersfield Oil Co., Santa Ana, capital, $200,000; par value, $1.00.
Samson Oil Co., Los Angeles, capital, $450,000; par value, $1.00.
St. Anthony Oil Co., Los Angeles, capital, $500,000; par value, $1.00.
Sespe Crude Oil Co., Los Angeles, capital, $500,000; par value, $1.00.
San Nicholas Oil Co., Los Angeles, capital, $1,000,000; par value, $10.00.
Simi Consolidated Oil Co., Ventura, capital, $300,000; par value, $1.00.
San Lorenzo Oil Co., Salinas, capital, $100,000; par value, $1.00.
Santa Fe Oil Co. of Stockton, Stockton, capital, $100,000; par value, $1.00.
Santa Maria Oil Co., McKittrick, capital, $250,000; par value, $1.00.
Sloc Oil Co., Los Angeles, capital, $600,000; par value, $1.00.
Swiss-American Oil & Development Co., San Francsico, capital, $200,000; par value, $1.00.
Sulphur Range Oil Co., Ventura, capital, $100,000; par value, $25.00.
Standard Crude Oil Developing Co., Los Angeles, capital, $500,000; par value, $1.00.
Standard Oil Co. of California, San Francisco, capital, $300,000; par value, $5.00.
Star Oil Co., Bakersfield, capital, $500,000; par value, $5.00.
Stockton Oil & Gas Co., Hanford, capital, $150,000; par value, $10.00.
Summit Oil Co., Visalia, capital, $128,000; par value, $5.00.
Summerland Land, Water & Oil Development Co., Kern, capital $100,000, par value, $1.00.
Sunset Oil Co., Santa Barbara, capital, $50,000; par value, $1.00.
Sun Oil & Petroleum Co., San Francisco, capital, $100,000; par value, $5.00.
Sunset Oil Mining & Development Co., San Francisco, capital, $500,000; par value, $1.00.
Sunset Crude Oil Co., San Francisco, capital, $1,000,000; par value, $1.00.
Sunbeam Oil Co., Los Angeles, capital, $150,000; par value, $100.00.
Sure-Shot Oil Co., Los Angeles, capital, $150,000; par value, $1.00.
Superior Oil Co., Bakersfield, capital, $500,000; par value, $1.00.
Success Oil Co., Los Angeles, capital, $1,000,000; par value, $10.00.
Shamrock Oil Co. Consolidated, San Francisco, capital, $500,000; par value, $1.00.
Sure-Shot Oil Producing Co., Reedley, capital, $100,000; par value, $1.00.
San Joaquin Valley Oil Co., Fowler, capital, $250,000; par value, $1.00.
Santa Paula Home Oil Co., Santa Paula, capital, $500,000; par value, $1.00.
Section Four Oil Co., Bakersfield, capital, $100,000; par value, $1.00.
San Francisco Petroleum Co., San Francisco, capital, $10,000,000; par value, $100.00.
San Francisco Natural Gas & Oil Co., San Francisco, capital, $1,000,000; par value, $10.00.
San Francisco Oil Mining Co., Los Angeles, capital, $300,000; par value, $1.00.
San Francisco Oil Co., San Francisco, capital, $144,000; par value, $100.00.
San Fernando Petroleum Co., San Francisco, capital, $700,000; par value, $50.00.
San Joaquin Petroleum Co., Bear Valley, capital, $1,500,000; par value, $50.00.
San Jose Petroleum Co., San Jose, capital, $1,000,000; par value, $100.00.
Santa Ana Petroleum Co., San Francisco, capital, $500,000; par value, $100.00.
Santa Barbara Oil Co., Santa Barbara, capital, $25,000; par value, $10.00.
Santa Barbara Oil & Mining Co., Santa Barbara, capital, $100,000; par value, $1.00.
Santa Clara Petroleum Co., Santa Clara, capital, $1,100,000; par value, $100.00.
Santa Clara Oil & Gold Co., Los Angeles, capital, $100,000; par value, $100,00.
Santa Paula Petroleum Co., San Francisco, capital, $500,000; par value, $10.00.
Santa Rosa Oil Co., San Luis Obispo, capital, $500,000; par value, $10.00.
Sespe Oil Co., Santa Paula, capital, $100,000; par value, $100.00.
Sisar Oil & Asphalt Co., Hueneme, capital, $200,000; par value, $100.00.
Smith & Bridgely Petroleum Co., Napa, capital, $1,600,000; par value, $100.00.
Solis Oil & Transportation Co., Gilroy, capital, $800,000; par value, $10.00.
South Pacific Oil Co., San Diego, capital, $6,000; par value, $100.00.
Southern California Oil & Supply Co., Los Angeles, capital, $50,000; par value, $10.00.
Sea Cliff Oil Mining Co., Los Angeles, capital, $120,000; par value, $30.00.
St. Petersburgh Petroleum Co., San Francisco, capital, $6,000,000; par value, $100.00.
Standard Oil Co. of California, San Francisco, capital, $2,500,000; par value, $50.00.
Stansbury, Petroleum Mining Co., Eureka, capital, $100,000; par value, $25.00.
Star Oil Works Co., San Francisco, capital, $1,000,000; par value, $100.00.
Star Consolidated Oil Co., San Francisco, capital, $500,000; par value, $1.00.
San Ramon Oi lCo., San Francisco, capital, $100,000; par value, $1.00.
Santa Clara Oil Co., Stockton, capital, $40,000; par value, $1.00;
Stanislaus Oil Co., Modesto, capital, $100,000; par value, $1.00.
Stanford Oil Co., San Francsico, capital, $100,000; par value, $1.00.
San Francisco Grocers' Oil Co., San Francisco, capital, $500,000; par value, $1.00.
Seacoast Land & Oil Co., Los Angeles, capital, $500,000; par value, $1.00.
Security Oil Co., Los Angeles, capital, $500,000; par value, $1.00.
Sartorial Oil Co., Los Angeles, capital, $500,000; par value, $1.00.
Stockton Sunset Oil Co., Stockton, capital, $500,000; par value, $1.00.
Sulphur Mountain Oil Development Co., Fullerton, capital, $300,000; par value, $1.00.
Southern California Commercial Travelers' Oil Co., Los Angeles, capital, $600,000; par value, $1.00.
Star Anticline Oil Co., Hollister, capital, $200,000; par value, $1.00.
Sultana Oil Co., Los Angeles, capital, $25,000; par value, $100.00.
Southern Oil Co., Pasadena, capital, $100,000; par value, $100.00.
Southern California Oil & Refining Co., Los Angeles, capital, $100.000; par value, $1.00.
San Diego Oil Belt Co., San Diego, capital, $100,000; par value, $50.00.

San Joaquin Valley Oil & Fuel Co., Fresno, capital, $2,000,000; par value, $100.00.
Santa Ana Oil Co., Santa Ana, capital, $50,000; par value, $10.00.
Selma Oil Co., Selma, capital $200,000; par value, $1000.00.
Silver Creek Petroleum Co., Fresno, capital, $200,000; par value, $1.00.
St. Lawrence Oil & Land Co., Hanford, capital, $50,000; par value, $10.00.
Sun Flower Oil Co., Hanford, capital, $100,000; par value, $1.00.
Sulphur Mountain Oil Co., Santa Ana, capital, $500,000; par value, $1.00.
Sunset Oil Co., Tulare, capital, $500,000, par value, $5.00.
Sunset Oil Co., Los Angeles, capital, $1,000,000; par value, $10.00.
San Benito Oil Co., San Jose, capital, $140,000; par value, $100.00.
Sacramento Petroleum Mining Co., Sacramento, capital, $256,000; par value, $100.00.
San Antonio Oil Co., Hueneme, capital, $100,-000; par value, $100.00.
San Carlos Oil Co., San Francisco, capital, $1,-000,000; par value, $10.00.
San Francisco Consolidated Oil Co., San Francisco, capital, $10,000,000; par value, $100.00.
Seaside Oil Co., Santa Barbara, capital, $200,-000; par value, $1.00.
San Pedro Oil Co., Los Angeles, capital, $500,-000; par value, $100.00.
Santa Barbara Oil & Mining Co., Santa Barbara, capital, $100,000; par value, $1.00.
Slocan Oil Co., Los Angeles, capital, $9,000; par value, $10.00.
Summerland Oil Development Co., Summerland, capital, $10,000; par value, $10.00.
Sunset Oil Co., Fresno, capital, $100,000; par value, $1.00.
Swan Oil Co., Visalia, capital, $15,000; par value, $1.00.
San Benito, Land & Oil Co., San Francisco, capital, $200,000; par value, $1.00.
San Cayetano Oil Co., Los Angeles, capital, $100,000; par value, $1.00.
Santa Fe Oil Co., San Francisco, capital, $1,030,-000; par value, $10.00.
San Emedio Oil Co., San Francisco, capital, $250,000; par value, $100.00.
San Francisco Oil Co., San Francisco, capital, $300,000; par value, $10,00.
San Luis Oil Co., Los Angeles, capital, $1,000,-000; par value, $100.00.
Tar Canyon Oil Co., San Francisco, capital, $100,000; par value, $1.00.
Temblor Oil & Developement Co., Bakersfield, capital, $104,000; par value, $1.00.
Temblor Oil & Development Co., Bakersfield, 000; par value, $10.00.
Tesla Oil Co., San Francisco, capital, $100,000; par value, $1.00.
Thirty Three Oil Co., San Francisco, capital, $500,000; par value, $5.00.
Tidal Wave Oil Co., San Francisco, capital, $250,000; par value, $5.00.
Tomboy Oil & Development Co., San Francisco, capital, $250,000; par value, $1.00.
Tres Sierritas Oil & Mining Co., Lemoore, capital, $600.000; par value, $5.00.
True Blue Oil Co., San Francisco, capital, $500,-000; par value, $5.00.
Tehachapi Oil & Development Co., Stockton, capital, $250,000; par value, $1.00.
Tapo Oil Co., Los Angeles, capital $500,000; par value, $1.00.
Telegraph Oil Co., Los Angeles, capital $500,-000; par value, $1.00.
Trojan Oil Co., Los Angeles, capital $600,000; par value, $1.00.
Tide Water Oil Co., San Francisco, capital, $1,500,000; par value, $5.00.
Trophy Oil Co., Los Angeles, capital, $500,000; par value, $1.00.
Trophy Oil Co., Coalinga, capital, $500,000; par value, $5.00.
Talisman Oil Co., San Francisco, capital, $30,-000; par value, $1.00.
Temple Crude Oil Co., Los Angeles, capital, $500,000; par value, $1.00.
Twenty Four Land & Oil Co., Hanford, capital, $250,000; par value, $1.00.
Twenty Seven Oil Co., San Francisco, capital, $80,000; par value, $10.00.
Tulare Lake Oil Co., San Francisco, capital, $100,000; par value, $100.00.
Twenty Eight Oil Co., Fresno, capital, $600,-000; par value, $10.00.
Tulare Oil & Mining Co., Tulare, capital, $300,-000; par value, $10.00.
Timber Canyon Oil Co., Santa Paula, capital, $20,000; par value, $100.00.
Turner Oil Co., Los Angeles, capital, $150,000; par value, $1.00.
Tapo Mining Co., Los Angeles, capital, $350,-000; par value, $1000.00.
Tousley Oil Co., Los Angeles, capital, $100,-000; par value, $2.00.
Tehama Oil Co., Tehama, capital, $100,000; par value, $10.00.
Trumbull Oil Co., San Francisco, capital, $150,-000; par value, $1.00.
Tower Oil Co., Tulare, capital, $250,000; par value, $1.00.
Tierra Oil Co., Los Angeles, capital, $300,000; par value, $1.00.
United Oil Co., San Francisco, capital, $1,000,-000; par value, $100.00.
Ukiah Oil Development Co., San Francisco, capital, $100,000; par value, $1.00.
Uncle Sam Oil Co., Los Angeles, capital, $300,-000; par value, $1.00.
Uncle Sam Oil & Development Co., San Francisco, capital, $500,000; par value, $5.00.
Union Jack Oil Co., Los Angeles, capital $1,-000,000; par value, $1.00.
United Brotherhood Petroleum Co., Oakland, capital, $100,000; par value, 50 cents.
U. S. Oil & Mining Co., Bakersfield, capital, $300,000; par value, $1.00.
Utica Oil Co., Fresno, capital, $200,000; par value, $5.00.
United Cons. Oil & Transportation Co., San Francisco capital, $1,000,000; par value, $10.00.
United Petroleum Co., Los Angeles, capital, $1,500,000; parvalue, $100.00.
Union Oil Co. of Cala., Santa Paula, capital, $5,000,000; par value, $100.00.
Union Petroleum Co., San Francisco, capital, $5,000,000; par value, $50.00.
United States Oil Co., San Jose, capital, $10,-000,000; par value, $100.00.
Uvas Creek Oil Co., San Francisco, capital, $500,000; par value, $500.00.
United States Petroleum Co., San Francisco, capital, $600,000; par value, $10.00.
United Oil Producers, San Francisco, capital, $1,000,000; par value, $50.00.
Vesta Oil Co., Los Angeles, capital, $300,000; par value, $1.00.
Vishnu Oil Co., San Francisco, capital, $500,-000; par value, $5.00.
Volcanic Oil Co., Los Angeles, capital, $500,-000; par value, $1.00.
Valley Oil Co., Los Angeles, capital, $500,000; par value, $1.00.
Venus Oil Co., San Francisco, capital, $100,-000; par value, $1.00.
Verona Oil Co., Hanford, capital, $150,000; par value, $1.00.
Victor Oil Co., San Francisco, capital, $500,-000; par value, $5.00.
Vicetas Oil Co., Selma, capital, $500,000; par value, $100.00.
Victory Oil Co., San Francisco, capital, $100,-000; par value, $1.00.
Virginia Oil Co., San Francisco, capital, $250,-000; par value, $2.50.
Volunteer Fireman Oil & Development Co., San Francisco, capital, $200,000; par value, $1.00.
Vandevier Petroleum Co., Fresno, capital, $250,-000; par value, $2.50.
Ventura Oil Co., Ventura, capital, $25,000; par value, $100.00.
Vesuvius Oil Co., Oakland, capital, $100,000; par value, $1.00.
Ventura Cons. Crude Oil Co., Los Angeles, capital, $1,000,000; par value, $1.00.
Vallecitos Oil & Development Co., San Francisco, capital, $250,000; par value, $1.00.
Ventura Oil Co., Los Angeles, capital, $200,-000; par value, $5.00.
Visalia Oil & Petroleum Co., Visalia, capital, $500,000; par value, $1.00.
Victoria Oil Co., Fresno, capital, $60,000; par value, $10.00.

Visalia Oil Co., Visalia, capital, $50,000; par value, $10.00.
Western Land and Oil Co. of Hanford, Hanford, capital, $250,000; par value, $1.00.
Western Land & Oil Syndicate, San Francisco, capital, $100,000; par value, $1.00.
Western Star Oil & Mining Co., Bakersfield, capital, $100,000; par value, $1.00.
West Side Oil Co., Fresno, capital, $100,000; par value, $10.00.
West Shore Oil Co., Oakland, capital, $20,000; par value, $5.00.
Westlake Rommel Oil Co., Los Angeles, capital, $250,000; par value, $25.00.
West Shore Oil Co. Cons., San Francisco, capital, $100,000; par value, $1.00.
Wheatville Oil Co., Wheatville, capital, $28,000; par value, $2.00.
White Creek Oil & Mineral Co., Hanford, capital, $250,000; par value, $1.00.
White Range Oil Co., San Francisco, capital, $100,000; par value, $1.00.
White Star Oil Co., Fresno, capital, $250,000; par value, $1.00.
Washington Petroleum Co., Hanford, capital, $250,000; par value, $2.50.
Western Ojai Land & Oil Co., Los Angeles, capital, $700,000; par value, $1.00.
Western Slope Oil Co., Los Angeles, capital, $300,000; par value, $1.00.
Western Star Oil & Coal Co., Los Angeles, capital, $350,000; par value, $1.00.
Whittier Cons. Oil Co., capital, $1,000,000; par value, $1.00.
Whittier & Kern River Oil Co., Los Angeles, capital, $300,000; par value, $1.00.
Whittier Oil & Development Co., Whittier, capital, $250,000; par value, $1.00.
Wolverine Oil Co., San Francisco, capital, $100,000; par value, $1.00.
Western Home Oil Co., Los Angeles, capital, $500,000; par value, $1.00.
Western Union Oil Co., Los Angeles, capital, $1,000,000; par value, $100.00.
Western Oil Co., Fresno, capital, $50,000; par value, $100.00.
Western Union Oil Co., San Francisco, capital, $350,000; par value, $1.00.
West Side Kern Oil Co., San Francisco, capital, $250,000; par value, $2.50.
Western Oil & Refining Co., San Francisco, capital, $500,000; par value, $5.00.
Walker Oil Co., Santa Barbara, capital, $200,000; par value, $10.00.
West Coast Oil Co., Los Angeles, capital, $250,000; par value, $1.00.
West Coast Oil Co., San Francisco, capital, $1,120,000; par value, $20.00.
West End Oil Co., Los Angeles, capital, $100,000; par value, $50.00.
Woodbury Oil Co., San Francisco, capital, $100,000; par value, $100.00.
Washington Oil Co., Los Angeles, capital, $5,000,000; par value, $1.00.
Waverly Oil Co., Hanford, capital, $250,000; par value, $1.00.
Wellington Oil Co., Los Angeles, capital, $250,000; par value, $1.00.
West Lake Oil Co., Los Angeles, capital, $500,000; par value, $1.00.
Warner Oil Co., Whittier, capital, $200,000; par value, $1.00.
Windsor Oil Co., Los Angeles, capital, $500,000; par value, $1.00.
White Mountain Oil Co., Tulare, capital, $1,000,000; par value, $1.00.
Wisconsin Oil Co., Fresno, capital, $150,000; par value, $1.00.
Wild Goose Oil Co.San Francisco, capital, $500,000; par value, $5.00.
Waterman Oil Land & Impvt. Co., San Francisco, capital, $350,000; par value, $1.00.
X Ray Oil Co., Selma, capital, $500,000; par value, $1.00.
Yellow Jacket Oil & Mining Co., Newman, capital, $200,000; par value, $1.00.
Zenith Oil Co., Los Angeles,, capital, $100,000; par value, $1.00.

List of all Oil Companies Incorporated in the Territory of Arizona.

The Laws of the Territory of Arizona Require a Corporation to Maintain a Place of Business there. For this reason many of the Companies have the address given in Arizona, although all their business is transacted in California. Where the California address is not given the publisher was unable to obtain the same at the time of going to press.

Aquila Oil & Mineral Co., Los Angeles, capital, $500,000; par value, $1.00.

Avocu Oil & Water Co., Phoenix, capital, $100,000; par value, $1.00.

American Oil Co., Phoenix, capital, $600,000; par value, $1.00.

American Girl Oil Co., Los Angeles, capital, $300,000; par value, $1.00.

Buena Ventura Oil Co., Los Angeles, capital, $500,000; par value, $1.00.

Brea Canyon, Santa Ana Canyon & Kern River Oil Co., capital, $190,000; par value, $1.00.

California Consolidated Petroleum Co., Los Angeles, capital, $5,000,000; par value, $1.00.

Climax Oil Co., Tucson, capital, $250,000; par value, $1.00.

California Mineral Oil Co., Los Angeles, capital, $500,000; par value, $1.00.

California Oil & Gas Co. of Arizona, Los Angeles, capital, $2,000,000; par value, $1.00.

California Oil Co., Los Angeles, capital, $1,000,000; par value, $1.00.

Coalinga Cons. Oil Co. Los Angeles, capital, $550,000; par value, $1.00.

Castaic Oil Development Co., Los Angeles, capital, $500,000; par value, $1.00.

California Crude Oil Co., Los Angeles, capital, $3,000,000; par value, $1.00.

Diamond Star Oil Co., Los Angeles, capital, $250,000; par value, $1.00.

Dominion Crude Oil Co., Los Angeles, capital, $1,000,000; par value, $1.00.

Eureka Crude Oil Co., Los Angeles, capital, $200,000; par value, $1.00.

Encinitas Oil Co., Yuma, capital, $500,000; par value, $1.00.

Elaine Oil Co., Phoenix, capital, $1,000,000; par value, $1.00.

Eastern Empire Oil Co., Los Angeles, capital, $200,000; par value, $1.00.

Fullerton Oil Co., Los Angeles, capital, $600,000; par value, $1.00.

Federal Oil & Development Co., Tucson, capital, $150,000; par value, $1.00.

Flagstaff Oil Co., Flagstaff, capital, $200,000; par value, $1.00.

Fearless Oil & Water Co., Phoenix, capital, $500,000; par value, $1.00.

Grapevine Canyon Oil Co., Los Angeles, capital, $150,000; par value, $1.00.

Globe Oil Co., Los Angeles, capital, $600,000; par value, $1.00.

Hawkeye State Oil Co., Los Angeles, capital, $500,000; par value, $1.00.

Howard Oil Co., Tucson, capital, $250,000; par value, $1.00.

Hard Cash Oil Co., Tucson, capital, $250,000; par value, $1.00.

Home Security Oil Co., Phoenix, capital, $500,000; par value, $1.00.

International Oil Co., Los Angeles, capital, $500,000; par value, $1.00.

Inter Nos Oil & Developement Co., Phoenix, capital, $400,000; par value, $1.00.

Industrial Oil Co., Los Angeles, capital, $750,000; par value, $1.00.

Iola Oil & Development Co., Los Angeles, capital, $250,000; par value, $1.00.

Kern River Oil Co., Los Angeles, capital, $200,000; par value, $1.00.

Kohinoor Oil & Refining Co., Los Angeles, capital, $1,000,000; par value, $1.00.

Los Angeles & Bakersfield Oil & Development Co., Los Angeles, capital, $200,000; par value, $1.00.

Lawyers & Bankers Oil Co., Los Angeles, capital, $1,000,000; par value, $1.00.

Lion Oil Co., Phoenix, capital, $500,000; par value, $1.00.

Long Beach Oil & Water Co., Phoenix, capital, $200,000; par value, $1.00.

Los Angeles & Kern Co. Oil Co., Los Angeles, capital, $250,000; par value, $1.00.

Metropolitan Oil Co., Los Angeles, capital, $750,000, par value, $1.00.

Monarch Oil Co., Los Angeles, capital, $500,000; par value, $1.00.

Newhall Oil Co., Los Angeles, capital, $300,000; par value, $1.00.

National Crude Oil Co., Los Angeles, capital, $1,000,000; par value, $1.00.

National Oil Co., Yuma, capital, $500,000; par value, $1.00.

Nickel Plate Oil Co., Phoenix, capital, $500,000; par value, $1.00.

Navajo Oil Co., Los Angeles, capital, $600,000; par value, $1.00.

New York Oil & Mining Co., Phoenix, capital, $500,000; par value, $1.00.

Ohio Oil & Development Co., Los Angeles, capital, $250,000; par value, $1.00.

Oak Grove Oil Co., Tucson, capital, $600,000; par value, $1.00.

Old Glory Oil Co., Los Angeles, capital, $500,000; par value, $1.00.

Oceanside Oil Co., Los Angeles, capital, $375,000; par value, $1.00.

Panochito Oil Co., Phoenix, capital, $500,000; par value, $1.00.

Pacific Crude Oil Co., Tucson, capital, $1,000,000; par value, $1.00.

Portland Oil Co., Los Angeles, capital, $500,000; par value, $1.00.

Puritan Oil Co., Los Angeles, capital, $200,000; par value, $1.00.

Puente Crude Oil Co., Los Angeles, capital, $500,000; par value, $1.00.

Providence Oil Co., Yuma, capital, $150,000; par value, $1.00.

Petroleum Producers Co. of Cala., Tucson, capital $250,000; par value, $1.00.

Pittsburg Cons. Oil Co., Phoenix, capital, $750,000; par value, $1.00.

Phoenix Oil & Fuel Co. of San Francisco, capital, $600,000; par value, $1.00.

Rock Creek Oil Co., Los Angeles, capital, $600,000; par value, $1.00.

Rimpau Oil Co., Los Angeles, capital, $500,000; par value, $1.00.

Rincon Crude Oil Co., Phoenix, capital, $200,000; par value, $1.00.

Sunset Petr. & Refining Co., Los Angeles, capital, $2,500,000; par value, $1.00.

Sunset King Oil Co., Los Angeles, capital, $300,000; par value, $1.00.

Summerland Oil & Mining Co., Phoenix, capital, $1,000,000; par value, $1.00.

Santa Barbara & Naples Oil & Land Co., Tucson, capital, $500,000; par valne, $1.00.

State Crude Oil Co., Los Angeles, capital, $500,000; par value, $1.00.

Sentinel Oil Co., Los Angeles, capital, $500,000; par value, $1.00.

Soquel Oil Co., Los Angeles, capital, $500,000, par value, $1.00.

Sunset Diamond Oil Co., Los Angeles, capital, $1,000,000; par value, $1.00.

San Diego Oil Co., Yuma, capital, $500,000; par value, $1.00.

Sterling Oil Co., Los Angeles, capital, $850,000; par value, $1.00.

San Diego Lion Oil Co., Prescott, capital, $200,000; par value, $1.00.

Santa Maria Oil Co., Los Angeles, capital, $500,000; par value, $1.00.

Seanta Oil Co., Phoenix, capital, $500,000 par value, $1.00.

Secu [illegible] Co., Los Angeles, capital, $500,000; par value, $1.00.

Sycamore Canyon Oil Co., Tucson, capital, $250,000; par value, $1.00.

Section 6 Oil Co., Phoenix, capital, $300,000; par value, $1.00.

Sunset Czar Oil Co., Los Angeles, capital, $500,000; par value, $1.00.

Three States Oil Co., Los Angeles, capital, $1,000,000; par value, $1.00.

The Good Hope Oil & Mining Co., Prescott, capital, $300,000; par value, $1.00.

The Commonwealth Oil & Mining Co., Los Angeles, capital, $125,000; par value, $1.00.

The Coast Range Oil & Mineral Co., Los Angeles, capital, $100,000; par value, $1.00.

The Southern Cross Oil Co., Tucson, capital, $1,000,000; par value, $1.00.

Vulcan Crude Oil Co., Prescott, capital, $300,000; par value, $1.00.

Ventura Petr. Mining Co., Yuma, capital, $200,000; par value, $1.00.

Woman's Pacific Coast Oil Co., Los Angeles, capital, $300,000; par value, $1.00.

Western Coast Oil Co., Yuma, capital, $1,000,000; par value, $1.00.

Yosemite Oil Co., Tucson, capital, $1,000,000; par value, $1.00.

Yankee Doodle Oil Co., Los Angeles, capital, $500,000; par value, $1.00.

*List of oil companies incorporated in Arizona and doing business in the State of California.

Places of Amusement in Los Angeles

Mojonier, Photographer.

CORONATION SCENE IN "PRISONER OF ZENDA," PRESENTED BY THE OLIVER-LESLIE CO.

MOROSCO'S BURBANK THEATER—Oliver Morosco, Lessee

Is near the leading hotels of the city, and offers its patrons exceptionally good attractions at popular prices. This is a cosy place in which to pass an evening.

ORPHEUM

The Fashionable Vaudeville Theater of Los Angeles

First and Main Streets.

Every night. Matinees Wednesdays, Saturdays and Sundays.
Best Seats, 25 cents at matinees; best reserved seats at night, 25 and 50 cents.

Blanchard Hall, 223 S. BROADWAY opposite City Hall

Is the Handsomest Music and Art Building in the West

Auditorium, seating 800, can be engaged for Musicales, Receptions, Lectures, Dances, etc. Rehearsal and Lecture Rooms for rent. Forty Studios—single and en suite. Public Art Gallery open daily, 1 to 4 p. m.

For any information apply to

F. W BLANCHARD

The Los Angeles Theater

227 South Spring Street

Is playing only

First-Class Combinations

Spotted something that isn't quite right?

Let us know and we'll fix it for future reprints. And as a thank you for your diligence, we'll send you a free Sothis book of your choice.

publisher@sothis.press

This page intentionally left blank

Made in the USA
Monee, IL
08 November 2026

68089562R00100